CONFESSIONS OF A
FILM INVESTOR

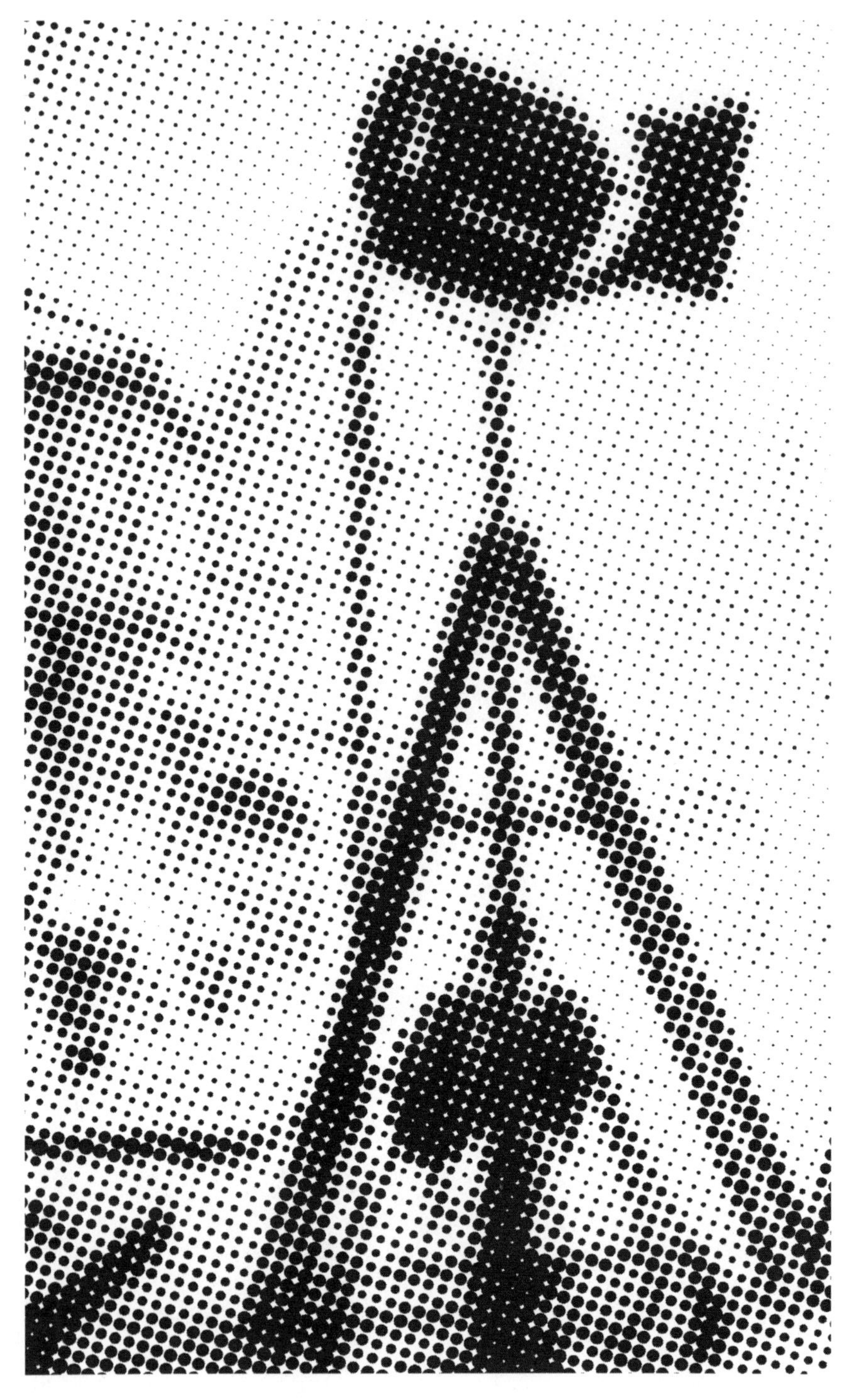

CONFESSIONS OF A
FILM INVESTOR

THE MISSING BOOK FOR INDEPENDENT FILMMAKERS

ALBERT SANDOVAL

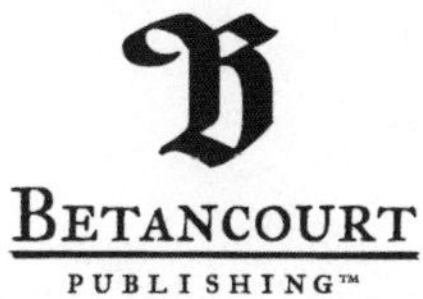

BETANCOURT
PUBLISHING™

To my wife and best friend, for your endless love, support, dedication, inspiring tenacity, and the smile that warms my heart every day.

To my talented and amazing children, for your loving support while being the toughest crowd around, and for always holding me to a higher standard. Dreams do come true!

To my loving grandparents, who raised me as their own. Thank you for always believing in me, making me believe in myself, and showing me how to love unconditionally. I miss you dearly.

DISCLAIMER

The information provided in this book is not intended to replace or serve as a substitute for any legal, tax, or other professional advice, consultation, or service. The prospective investor should consult with a professional in the respective legal, tax, accounting, or other professional area before making any decisions or entering into any contracts pertaining to anything described herein.

Each investor is encouraged to review and evaluate investments at the investor's own discretion and determine, at their own discretion, the appropriateness of making the particular investment. The author of this book strongly encourages each investor to complete their own due diligence with licensed professionals, such as a CPA and attorney, prior to making any investment, and will not offer any legal nor tax advice.

Copyright © 2019 Albert Sandoval

Confessions of a Film Investor

written by Albert Sandoval

First Edition

Published by:

Betancourt Publishing

Cover Art by:

Albert Sandoval

All rights reserved.

ISBN: 978-1-7338329-1-5

www.BetancourtPublishing.com

Printed in the U.S.A.

CONFESSIONS OF A
FILM INVESTOR

CONTENTS

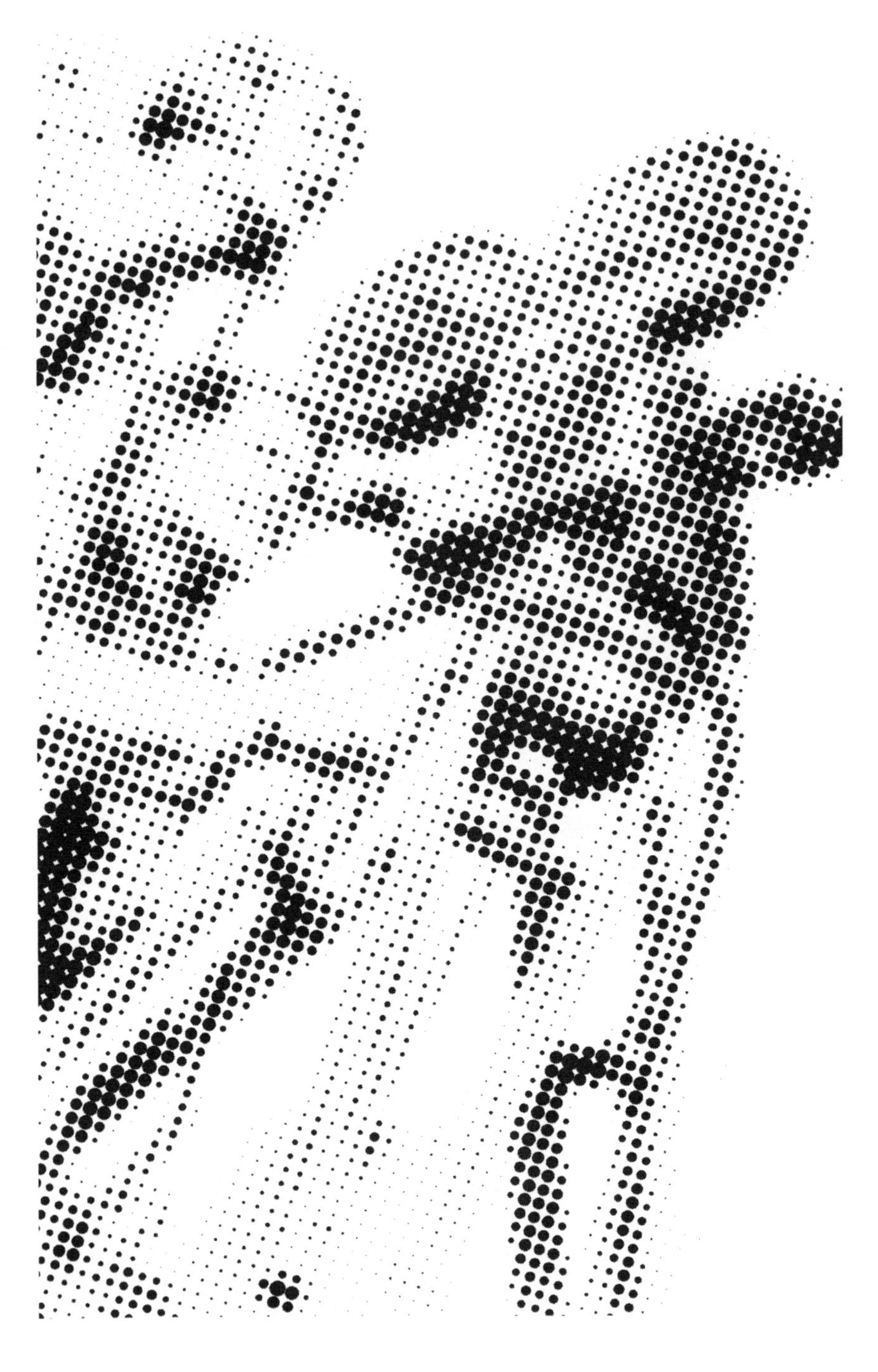

IT'S YOUR TIME TO TAKE ACTION

"You have fallen in love with an impossible medium because it's so hard to get the money for your pictures, and it's so hard to get the distribution."

—Orson Welles

Once upon a time, in a magical world called Hollywood, there lived a mythical creature known as a film investor. Very few people knew what this creature looked like, but almost everyone in this mystical place was searching for one, for the investor held a magic checkbook that could make dreams come true.

Most of these creatures called film investors did not have any markings to distinguish them as such, for they live ordinary lives: they were doctors, lawyers, business owners, real estate investors, and everything else imaginable. So how could the people know these creatures from ordinary mortals? What should they say to get them to open those magic checkbooks?

We have all faced adversities in different forms: we have all loved, we have all lost, and we have all created something from nothing. I am convinced more than ever that anyone can accomplish their wildest fantasies of success by rewiring their thinking against the conditioning of modern society and by taking action.

Napoleon Hill famously said, "There is one quality which one must possess to win, and that is definiteness of purpose, the knowledge of what one wants, and a burning desire to possess it." Armed with knowledge, a mastery of your craft and an unwavering determination, anyone can succeed at anything they set their mind to accomplish.

As a filmmaker, I believe there is value in sharing our experiences, particularly those that have resulted in finding these mythical creatures. There has never been a better time to be an independent filmmaker, and I believe we are at the threshold of a new golden era of cinema.

Let's make history!

THE BUG

THIS BOOK IS FOR YOU IF...

If you're reading this, you probably have the filmmaker's bug; actually, it's more like a disease that will never go away. Against all logic and reason—everything inside of you is saying it is impractical to pursue a life in independent filmmaking—and still, there is nothing else in the world you are capable of thinking about or doing. That is the dedication and passion required to make anything happen, especially in this business. There is nothing glamorous or practical about our world. This business will suck you dry of everything you have to give, it will take years off your life, and it will make you question your sanity over and over again.

You will meet the absolute worst human beings who walk the face of the earth, as this business seems to attract more lunatics than any other industry in the world. You will likely go broke, you will go crazy, and you will need a support system that will keep you standing as everything and everyone kicks you down at every turn. You will be rejected and discouraged, constantly. Your films will likely not change the world and will probably not make you rich.

They may not teach you this in film school, and most people don't write about this. It is the nasty, ugly, despicable world of independent film. It is not an art form that allows you to work alone, like painting or landscape photography; this art form requires many people to align their interests with yours while working toward the same goal, and it needs lots of money and time. You will beg, borrow, and steal, and you will pay with blood, sweat, and tears. There is no better way to say it. However, if you have the bug and you don't make movies, you will regret it for the rest of your life.

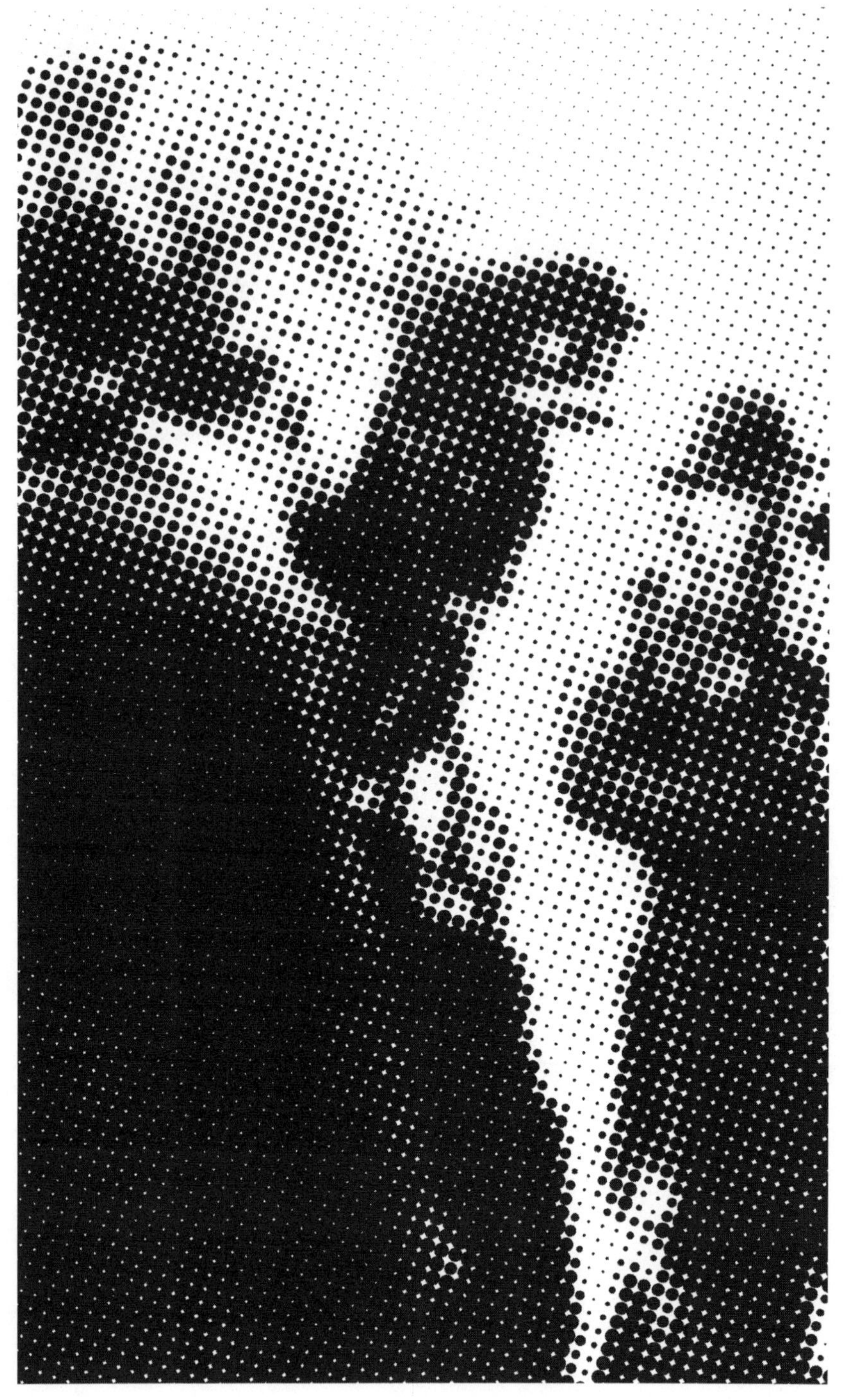

MY MANIFESTO

"Birds born in a cage think flying is an illness."

—Alejandro Jodorowsky

As human beings, we form ideas and create fantasies that ultimately define specific aspects of reality for each of us. These fantasies can be most evident when we are children. Maybe it was a dream of being a superhero, a racecar driver, or professional athlete, or perhaps it was as simple as having a bedroom of your own or becoming a film director. However straightforward and simple our ideas, they always begin as fantasies.

For many of you, the concept of finding an investor who will believe in you enough to give you the cash you need to make your movie is and remains in the realm of fantasy. How do these people look? What do they say? What should you say to them?

To add to the mysterious illusion, the film industry is a minefield of bullshit, with many unscrupulous characters preying on those who have little or no experience dealing with real players. These people are projections of what they (and, in many cases, any of us) might believe a real investor looks like—maybe it's the car, the suit, or the fancy watch. Think of the "rich character" trope used in children's cartoons and tongue-in-cheek comedies. The fat guy in a black pin-striped suit, a top hat, with suspenders, a cane, and shiny wingtips, smoking a cigar. Without using any words or another context, when we see that image, we know what it is representing. As grown-ups, I think we can all agree this stereotype is not reality; it is nothing more than a manifestation of our collective fantasies.

I learned a long time ago that everyone in the film business generally ends up in one of two categories. The *talkers* are those who spend all of their time making noise but never really accomplish anything significant. The *doers*, on the other hand, ultimately master their dreams. My goal is to teach you how to be a *doer* and achieve your goals.

CHASING YESTERDAY'S BUSINESS MODELS IN A RACE TO THE BOTTOM

The existing independent film business often relies on a web of complex financing structures, and no two films are ever financed in quite the same way. Finding financing in this structure usually means relying on "experts" who attempt to intellectualize and justify the value of a film prior to production, utilizing historical sales data that is rarely ever accurate. With a script, a director, and a "bankable" cast, a producer might start raising money with pre-sales, debt, maybe some equity, a gap partner, some incentives, and perhaps a deferred post deal to piece together the capital they need over some painfully long period that will often involve many people. Lenders, sales agents, distributors, and probably a bond company will put producers under their own set of stringent terms.

While private investors will often play a part in this puzzle, I do not believe this complex structure is an optimal way to get most investors interested in being a part of your film. I have seen these complex structures scare real investors away from a project more often than not. A few years ago, I planned to meet a foreign investor for dinner. This would not be our first meeting, but I had already determined he was a real investor and I had spent time developing our relationship and provided value by educating him on the industry as much as possible. He was in town for a few days, so I took him to his favorite steakhouse in Beverly Hills. Halfway through our glass of Macallan 25, he disclosed to me that he had met a few other production companies prior to making the decision to work with me. He seemed disenchanted by the other companies, so I asked him specifically what it was he didn't like about them. He answered with one word, in a heavy Eastern European accent: "Shit." One word was all it took for me to understand exactly what he meant. After digging a bit more, I learned that he had been pitched various versions of complex financing structures that made him feel like the companies were trying to take advantage of him by using descriptions he didn't understand.

The forces in the existing independent film business are desperate to preserve their place in the ecosystem because their value is being challenged for the first time in decades. These experts are protective of the systems they have controlled for so many years. Meanwhile, new business models forged by Netflix, Amazon, and other streaming platforms don't have a significant place in this existing structure of raising money before production—a further indication that growth opportunities may not be in these old models. Change is painful for everyone and often impossible for some to accept. As a result, we are witnessing a significant and unprecedented paradigm shift in the industry. The music industry experienced this correction years ago, while the movie business has remained artificially propped up by blockbuster event films. Once a film is complete, monetization has been supplemented by platforms like Netflix and Amazon pouring billions of dollars into the marketplace, reinforcing the illusion that there is a strong future in these old ways of doing business.

To make things worse, there are many self-proclaimed "experts" creating podcasts and online videos spewing regurgitated information they read in some outdated book, or maybe they heard some filmmaker mention in an interview. These people are generally not real players in the business, and they spread misinformation while feeding on each other in an echo chamber of bullshit. Unfortunately, we have probably all listened to or watched one of these videos, and maybe even believed we learned something from them. It is the strangest thing to watch them speak with such authority when, in many cases, their IMDB profile alone is an indication they are not qualified to be giving the advice. I think some of these people genuinely mean well, but they're just unaware that the information they are providing is entirely dead wrong. In fairness, the speed at which industry changes are happening makes things difficult to follow, even for those of us in the trenches.

I believe there is a massive disconnect between independent filmmakers and investors, a separation rooted in most filmmakers' ignorance about money people. I am writing this book as both a private investor and filmmaker who has invested, and partnered with other investors, in equity and debt financing for a variety of film projects that challenge conventional practices. This isn't a book on film production, the business of film financing, or the various complex structures that currently exist. I will share with you the mistakes I frequently witness when filmmakers (including some veteran producers) go looking for funding from private investors. I will share firsthand accounts of my search for financing, what I have seen work, and what I believe will never work in what is a newly emerging global business.

I believe change creates excellent opportunities, and smart, entrepreneurial thinkers know this. Change also comes with difficult decisions, especially the ones that make us face our obsolescence. When a new technology called television was invented, there were movie studios who chose not to embrace the platform and instead resisted the change, and in a relatively short time, their businesses suffered. Some went from being top film studios to bankruptcy.

The industrial age and publicly traded companies drove mass market global thinking. Madison Avenue, Wall Street, and Main Street followed this pattern, and the snowball got bigger and bigger. Consumers have been conditioned to buy "popular" brands, creating a value system based on "bigger" and "more," in a pattern of perpetual and virtually limitless growth. Hollywood grew more dependent on this global financial ecosystem as the major studios were gobbled up by massive multinational media conglomerates, and new business models have been built upon larger and larger segments of consumers. Then came the narrative of "too big to fail" that was pushed on us as Wall Street and the banking industry were bailed out by the U.S. Government in 2008. The artificial growth pattern continued, fueled by inflation, consumption, and debt. Another excellent example of this is the increasing cost of attending university in the U.S., which is now comparable to buying a house, leaving young adults and their parents deeply in debt before young people even leave the starting line.

We've gone from keeping up with the Joneses to keeping up with the Kardashians as entertainment, news, and advertising media have played a significant role in the illusion of endless growth. Moviegoers now expect massive event films in major theaters, demanding business structures that can only exist interdependently with Wall Street, the banking industry, and global audiences. As a result, studios and producers have inadvertently allowed the Chinese government to impose its censorship requirements on American films. The U.S. is now dependent on China as a critical segment of the global market, and studios are creating content that is more aware of—or at least adaptable to—these censorship requirements. To add to the complicated business, piracy is a major problem worldwide as many other key markets are contracting.

I contend that we are in a state of change with an inevitably massive economic correction on the horizon. Artificial intelligence and the internet will no doubt continue to impact our business as automation will eventually replace the middleman in almost every sector of industry worldwide. A new value system is emerging, and with it, new ways of structuring a film to be profitable. I believe big talent, who at one time guaranteed a film's success, have lost their star power, and, in some cases, can even devalue a movie. The economics of the current film business are entirely out of alignment with the realities of the market. As talent agents demand yesterday's rates and the middlemen continue to feed on the scraps of what once was, forming under all of this is an unprecedented opportunity to be a part of a newly emerging Hollywood business.

I will no doubt ruffle some feathers with some of what I say, but as an entrepreneur, I have learned the value of remaining platform-agnostic, particularly during times of rapid change, with the latitude to expand, contract, or refine my strategies at any time. Our business is no longer a "destination." We are on a fast-moving train in a world filled with rapidly developing technologies that will directly impact us all.

Modern audiences celebrate "labels" and what makes each of us unique, and as micro-niche groups become mainstream, it is becoming nearly impossible to predict what will be successful on a global scale. Unfortunately, as these changes are happening, Hollywood's measure of success has grown more dependent on its ability to capture global audiences.

Two roads have always existed: one path leading to a complex world of sales agents, pre-sales, casting, minimum guarantees, and gap financing, and another way that is genuinely independent—bootstrapping a project while grinding out the best film you can make for the least amount of money. Films like *El Mariachi* or *Clerks* made huge impacts on the market and the filmmakers' careers. My predictions are that we will see more growth in lower-budget films for niche audiences, and that we will continue to see current complex independent film financing crumble as existing business models prove to be less relevant in the rapidly changing film business.

There will always be a place for a "hit" movie in any genre and market, and I believe the other side of the rainbow for all of us will be when the event and franchise films run their course and studios focus more on smaller niche audiences. Streaming platforms like Netflix and Amazon are currently filling these gaps, and the viewers are going with them. If these platforms continue, they may take even more of a market share from the big studios, while these studios remain distracted by chasing worldwide hits. Netflix's and Amazon's models allow for a wider net, spread over many titles and an endless window of time, while the big studios might hang between life and death on one release, locked into predetermined windows dictated by old contracts with old favored-nation clauses and pressure from theatrical exhibitors to delay home entertainment releases.

As a fan of cinema, I believe a renaissance has begun. I think audiences have a growing appetite for non-event films with human stories. I feel the apocalyptic, CG-heavy, end-of-the-world stories—although very entertaining—are getting stale as a new generation of Hollywood is beginning to peek its head over the old crumbling business. As independent filmmakers, we have a responsibility to contribute to the coming golden age of cinema. Private film investors play a crucial role in making this happen, and we need to be open to new business models and standards while we educate, inspire, and promote the emerging film industry.

You may or may not know this, but many producers refer to private investments as "dumb money," not because the investor is dumb, but because the investor is ignorant to the complex nuances of the crazy existing film business. This is quite common in film investors and is becoming more common due to the information that is available online and in many books that continue to spread outdated, idealized, and romantic versions of the film business. As a producer, you should never take "dumb money"—it is your job to educate your investors and make them your business partners. Treat their money as if it is your own.

HOW I GOT INTO THIS BUSINESS

I was born and raised in the creative community of Silverlake, a well known district of Los Angeles, where Charlie Chaplin made his first film and Walt Disney opened his first studio. I lived, went to school, and walked almost daily by these historical sites. Growing up in the 1970s and '80s before moving image-making at home was widely accessible, I would only dream of making my own films. The idea was so ridiculously out of reach for me that I never actually considered it a serious career path and didn't dare say it aloud for fear of being ridiculed by my peers. I was conditioned to believe that if I found a "good" job, got married, bought a house, took a vacation once a year, and saved my money, life would be good. Getting a job, getting married, or moving out of the house as a young person was a coming of age. There was no place in this narrative to think about being a filmmaker—that was like trying to be a rockstar or an artist. The only rebels were my grandparents: they played a significant role in my childhood, and one of the things they always told me is that I could do and be whatever I wanted. I was crazy enough to believe them, thankfully.

In high school, I produced music in my bedroom studio and

worked part-time as a DJ for school dances, weddings, parties, and bar/bat mitzvahs. I also made money on the side as a photographer and an artist, mostly airbrushing clothing and cars in my mom's garage. I was so passionate about art that I arranged to arrive at school one to two hours early every day so that I could work on my art projects before class. My art teacher, Mrs. Bowen, was one of the most influential people in my life. She would often shake her finger at me and, among many other things, say, "You had better not waste that talent." She likely had no idea what an impact those words would have on me, even today.

Despite the forces of culture and society, I decided to go to art school, where I learned graphic design, what I thought would be the most practical use of my creative talent. The entry into my career as a creative professional was diverse. I learned professional photography working for a baby portrait studio, and eventually launched a full-blown career in fashion photography. My design skills landed me work at major studios, advertising agencies around the country, and ultimately as the owner and operator of my own agency.

In my early twenties, I got a job as Senior Art Director at an advertising agency in Los Angeles. I was new to the business, loaded with creative energy and had not yet been jaded. The agency was about to lose a significant client because they had not presented a campaign that the client liked. I stepped in and developed what I thought was the solution. The client loved it and my idea saved what I later discovered to be an account worth over $25M a year. My new team and I had to work over the holidays to meet the tight deadlines. There were rumors of holiday bonuses and I was anxiously expecting to see if they were true. What would it be? $10,000? $25,000? Maybe more? Afterall, I saved a huge account. It was the afternoon of Christmas Eve, my team and I were hard at work, and the owner of the agency walked in. The tension built as he walked around the office with no emotion on his face. He eventually made it to my office and shook my hand, "happy holidays," he said, handed me an envelope, turned around and walked out. I waited a while to make sure he left the building, my anticipation grew and after several minutes I grabbed the envelope and ripped it open to find a check for what was around $3,000 ($5,000 less payroll taxes.)

In a swell of emotions, I didn't know what to think. Did I miss something? I couldn't understand how saving a $25-million-dollar piece of business wasn't worth more. I had worked my ass off to make it happen, I was away from my family for most of the holiday season and my team and I were working while the rest of the agency was on vacation. It was at that precise moment that I decided I was going to be the guy handing out the bonuses and not the one sitting and waiting for a pat on the back. That was the last 9-5 job I ever had.

All of my experiences have contributed to who I am as a business person and unbeknownst to me at the time, I was building an effective and relevant foundation for my entry into the independent film world.

In 2008, I started a side venture with one of the smartest business people I've ever met. He is a very successful investor, graduated at the top of his class at Wharton, and had a very efficiently run real estate empire with his sister. I had the privilege of spending over a year sitting in their offices in Brentwood (L.A.), going to business meetings with them, and participating in negotiations and strategic planning. I had a very rare insider's view of their successful operation. What I realize now is that this was my business school, and maybe even better than an MBA. To this day, they probably don't understand what an impact they had on me, and they're likely not even aware that some of the most common and seemingly simple conversations were meaningful learning experiences for me. They became my mentors, and I learned how "money people" think, how they perceive risk and how they plan their successes one step at a time and in great detail. Unfortunately, I started working with them after I had made some bad real estate investments on my own. Fortunately, I was there to watch them react to the economic downturn, which they survived completely unscathed. These lessons couldn't have come at a better time, as I was beginning to find my way after the massive financial blow. I used that negative experience to drive me harder every day. I turned that energy into a passion for whatever it was I was doing, one day at a time. I never stopped plugging away at every available opportunity, and I believed I was at the forefront of something massive.

This chapter of my life taught me that everything could be lost in an instant. I realized that although I had a wonderful time running my creative agency, I had compromised on my real dream of making movies. I understood that the concept of "security" was more of an illusion, and that we are all vulnerable to losing anything at any time, and if we get comfortable with what we have, it will eventually dry up. It is never about what you have or have made; it is always about what you can make yourself, at any time and under any circumstances.

I remember the day as if it was yesterday. As we watched the financial world crumbling on TV, I turned to my wife, Diana, and said, "I'm going to make movies." When I think about this today, I wonder how in the world she kept a straight face and didn't tell me I was out of my mind. Instead, she said, "Do it," and she meant it. My wife has always been my rock. She is my inspiration. Everything I've accomplished in my life has started with her believing in me, and that was all I needed.

By this time, I had already started RadioactiveGiant as a consulting company, mostly for consumer electronic brands who were transforming from sheet-metal companies to digital content platforms. I was also taking meetings at studios, and I remember the looks on the faces of C-level executives when I told them people would soon be watching movies on their phones. I realized it was probably very much like the music industry with early predictions of trading music over the internet. I came to the reality that there was a massive change coming, and it was at that moment that I was determined to build an independent film studio for the future of the business as I saw it. By 2010, I began prioritizing the film production part of my business and searched for the right investor-partners.

By 2011, I raised my first round of outside financing, which launched RG as a well established independent film production and distribution studio. Thankfully, the business skills and expertise I'd learned in my earlier business life proved useful in the film industry. Rather than following the crowd and doing the same thing everyone else was doing, I found a path up the back of the mountain that led me to success. My skills as an entrepreneur and investor took priority over my creative background. There are very talented creative people in this industry, but few who are gifted in the business side. I didn't want to compete on the same level as everyone else. My instincts led me away from the "industry" crowd, and I have instead focused on developing meaningful relationships with real players who are more aligned with my way of doing business and creating real value. I learned early on that if you are not first, you must be different, and most importantly, that meant being disruptive.

I am thrilled with the decision I made in 2008, and my only regret is that it took that long for me to pursue my real passion for filmmaking. This experience has reinforced that anyone can do anything if you set your mind to it. The 10,000-hour rule is real, and I've spent much more than that gaining the experience I have, learning from mentors, and learning every aspect of filmmaking from concept to completion. I have immersed myself in the film finance and global distribution world with a reliable network, and I am having the time of my life. Master your passions and your craft, and give your best always, and you will experience a great life with anything you choose to do.

I am now a principal film investor, entrepreneur and CEO of RadioactiveGiant. I have multiple companies in and out of the film industry. I manage my own financing initiatives and maintain a strong network of private investors around the world. The economic downturn in 2008 taught me the importance of thinking like a money person. In my case, completely changing my perspective to that of business and money was born out of necessity for survival. The business experiences throughout my career, all of my failures, and all of my successes have all led me to pursue my passion for filmmaking. I strive to build a network of likeminded people who respect and understand the business side of the art of cinema, and my goal is to be an active participant in what I believe to be an exciting new era of the film business.

WHY YOU NEED THIS BOOK

As the CEO of the production-distribution studio RadioactiveGiant, I have had the good fortune of sitting on both sides of the desk, as both an investor and as a filmmaker. They are not the same. I have been pitched thousands of times at film markets, festivals, and in line at the bank and grocery store. I receive film submissions almost daily from writers, agents, and attorneys. I have sat in front of people with decades of experience in the film business, and I am always amazed at how much almost everyone I meet entirely misses the mark on how to actually get a film funded in today's market.

There are MANY ways to finance a film. This book is about private film investors. It will not cover any specific financing structures. This book is NOT a film finance book teaching you how to structure your deals, but it will address what is likely the most critical piece to getting your independent film financed by any private investor.

I will cover things you may already know or have a strong opinion about, and I may say things you disagree with or that conflict with your own experiences. That's OK. I'm not writing this to give you all the answers; I certainly don't have them. I am writing this to share my experiences and what has worked for me to make movies—not just talk about making them, or spend years chasing money down a black hole, but actually produce and finance films in a matter of 2-3 years. Hopefully, any differences in our experiences will help light up a new perspective or idea.

This book is not intended to be a motivational book to make you feel all warm and fuzzy while you tackle the grand task of finding money to make your film. I will give it to you straight—no fluff, no bullshit—and you do with it what you want. Don't get lost in the crazy world of film financing without at least reading this book. I promise you won't regret it.

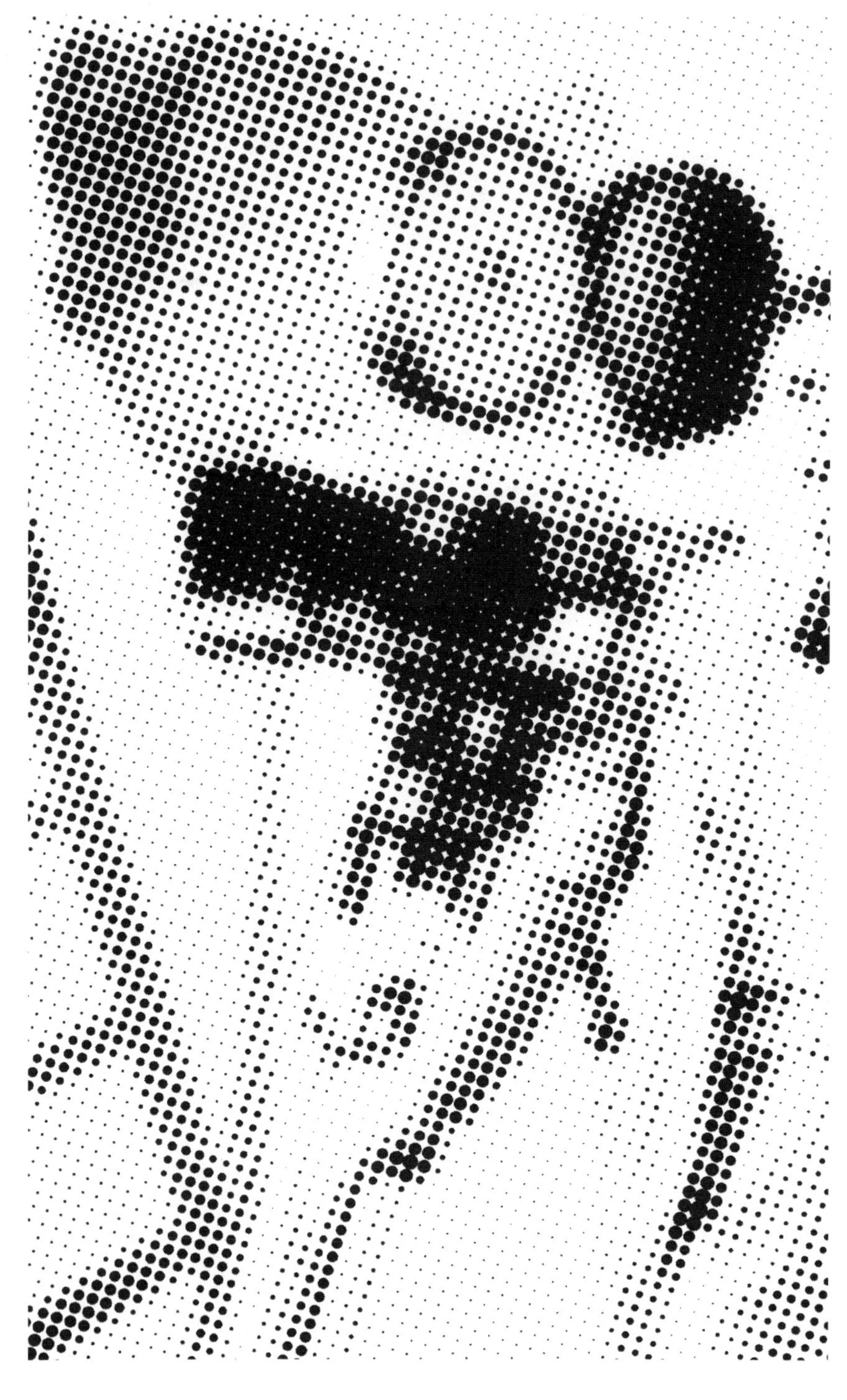

CHAPTER TWO

THE BUSINESS OF ART

*"We don't make movies to make money,
we make money to make more movies."*

—WALT DISNEY

Cinema is like no other art form in the world, and it is among the few disciplines that require many people focused on the same goal, lots of money, and a big audience willing to pay for the end product. The business side of art is too often overlooked or underestimated by the artists themselves, and there is instead a tendency to avert or pass those responsibilities off to a manager, agent, or even a partner or employee, trusting they will make the best business decisions on your behalf. Creative masters like Stanley Kubrick, David Bowie, and even Andy Warhol were great at business. They may have made some mistakes along the way (as we all do), but those mistakes made them proficient at their business, which allowed them, in turn, to accomplish everything they wanted as artists. It is essential to understand that art is a business like any other industry, and cinema is one of the most competitive categories of business. If you're not first, you must be different and disruptive if you want to survive.

I am an artist, music producer, photographer, writer, and film director, but I am always a businessman, first. Being creative does not mean you cannot excel at business, despite society's general view of artists with all of its outdated stereotypes. I believe society has been conditioned by false boundaries born out of the industrial age where workers were told to do one thing and do it well. This myth has been carried through western culture generation by generation, based on nothing more than a perceived economic need. This industrial experiment has gradually conditioned society to believe that we are capable of being good at only one thing. I'm here to tell you that anyone can master their craft as an artist and as a businessperson if they put in the time and effort necessary.

Filmmaking is a business, and you should always integrate business strategies with creative execution. Find efficiencies and develop strategic relationships with individuals and companies who have aligned interests. Making a movie gives you a powerful platform, and you should use it whenever possible. There are many types of investments, including some that don't involve money but bring measurable value to your bottom line. Trading goods and services for credits in the film is a great example. There are even service providers who may be willing to defer all or some of their fees.

Read, read, and read more. Business and finance books will give you an inside look at how money people think. They will inspire you to get creative with your deal making and may even give you specific ideas on how to reach your goals, or, at the very least, help you look at your challenges from a different perspective.

TAKE ACTION: GET YOUR BUSINESS MIND THINKING

• Find out if and when local service providers, crew, or desired cast have a part of the year where business slows down for them, and consider scheduling your production and post-production accordingly.

• Don't be afraid to ask service providers or some crew members if they are willing to defer any portion of their fees. You may find a great camera operator who needs a Director of Photography credit to take their career to the next level. They may agree to accept less money in exchange for the needed credit.

• A non-union actor may be seeking to become eligible to join the Screen Actors Guild (SAG-AFTRA), and the right talking role in your film may give them the eligibility they need.

• Consider registering your production with local colleges to recruit interns. Check local laws, and rules, and with any other participating labor unions, before making definite plans.

• Local businesses are great for negotiating in-kind or deeply discounted services in exchange for credits in your film. Meals, cars, locations, wardrobe, props, hotels—there is no end to the possibilities.

• In addition to states and countries, local municipalities (cities and counties) often have their own incentives to attract productions to their region. This could mean faster turnaround and low-cost or even free filming permits. You may even secure a great location at little to no cost. Leave no stone unturned, when it comes to finding these opportunities. They are everywhere.

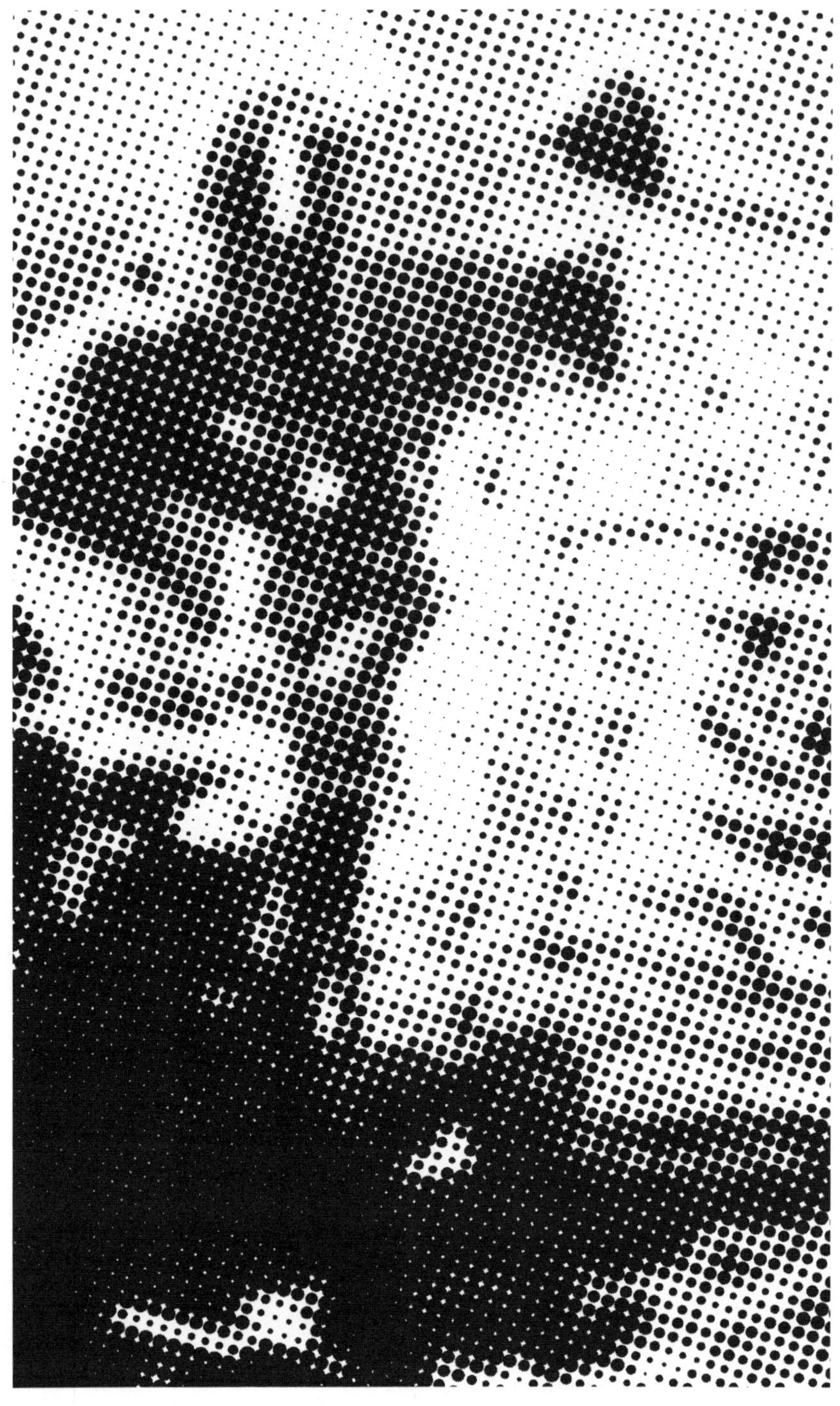

CHAPTER THREE

FILM SCHOOLS MAKE DIRECTORS, NOT PRODUCERS

"Experience is what you get while looking for something else."

—Federico Fellini

I have always been supportive of film schools, and I believe there's enormous value in building a network of like-minded filmmakers, learning different aspects of physical production, and having dedicated time and resources for hands-on filmmaking at school.

However, film schools make directors, not producers.

Very few film business courses cover the nasty, non-sugar-coated versions of our industry. You need to forget everything you learned in film school and become a real producer. Your job title is now CEO of your film project, and as CEO, you will be expected to be a frugal and responsible steward of the money, the schedule, and your team, all while fostering the best creative work possible and aligning the interests of 10, 50, 100, 200 or more crew members—all working together and towards the same goal. You will have terrible challenges, and you will need to fire people you like and hire people you don't. All while putting out wildfires. All without disrupting or compromising the quality of your production. All while juggling day-to-day operations.

Here's the straight truth about our industry as it stands today:

distribution for independent movies is very hard to come by. Acquisitions are driven by marketability. That means name value, name talent, name writer, director, and producer. Sadly, art has no value in the general film market. A film does have to be "good" to be acquired, but what do distributors look for when they acquire a film? The first thing they look for is a commercial project—something they already understand, and something that allows them to efficiently utilize historical sales data to project a return on their investment. They are not necessarily looking for a film that breaks new ground. If it is original, it should fill other proven commercial needs. Otherwise, a distributor will not know how to sell it.

A festival or major award-winning film does not guarantee success in the market. Acquisitions by distributors have become more of a pre-sales and production game. It is leaving very little room for our precious art films. Distributors know what they want, and they are in a constant state of reacting to market demand. Sometimes everyone is asking for horror, sometimes it's action, and sometimes it's romantic comedies. As smaller distributors move more into the production and management game, they have even more to lose on titles that don't perform well. Even smaller distributors are becoming much more selective about the films they take on.

The key is to think like a producer and emotionally detach yourself from the project. Learn to look at your project from an investor's perspective. An investor may not understand the subtext or subtle artistic nuances that make your script so unique. You are not writing for your professor or peers. Consider having a second "reader" version of your script with more narrative descriptions. Most private investors may not be seasoned script readers.

TAKE ACTION: THINK LIKE A PRODUCER

• Never ask an investor to sign an NDA (non-disclosure agreement) before pitching your project. This is the sign of an amateur, and does not communicate good faith.

• You need to be honest with yourself and find your optimal budget level. The level that will allow you to thrive and operate with the least amount of resistance: under-promise and over-deliver.

• Every successful entrepreneur understands the importance of defining success. Filmmaking is no different. It is your job as the producer to define success for yourself and your investors.

• The deal is always what matters most. The deal is more important than the budget amount or any of the creative elements of your project.

• Don't rely on your unique idea. Screenplays can be like reading a foreign language to some investors, and remember, there is no shortage of great ideas floating around. Don't compete on ideas alone, or you will lose.

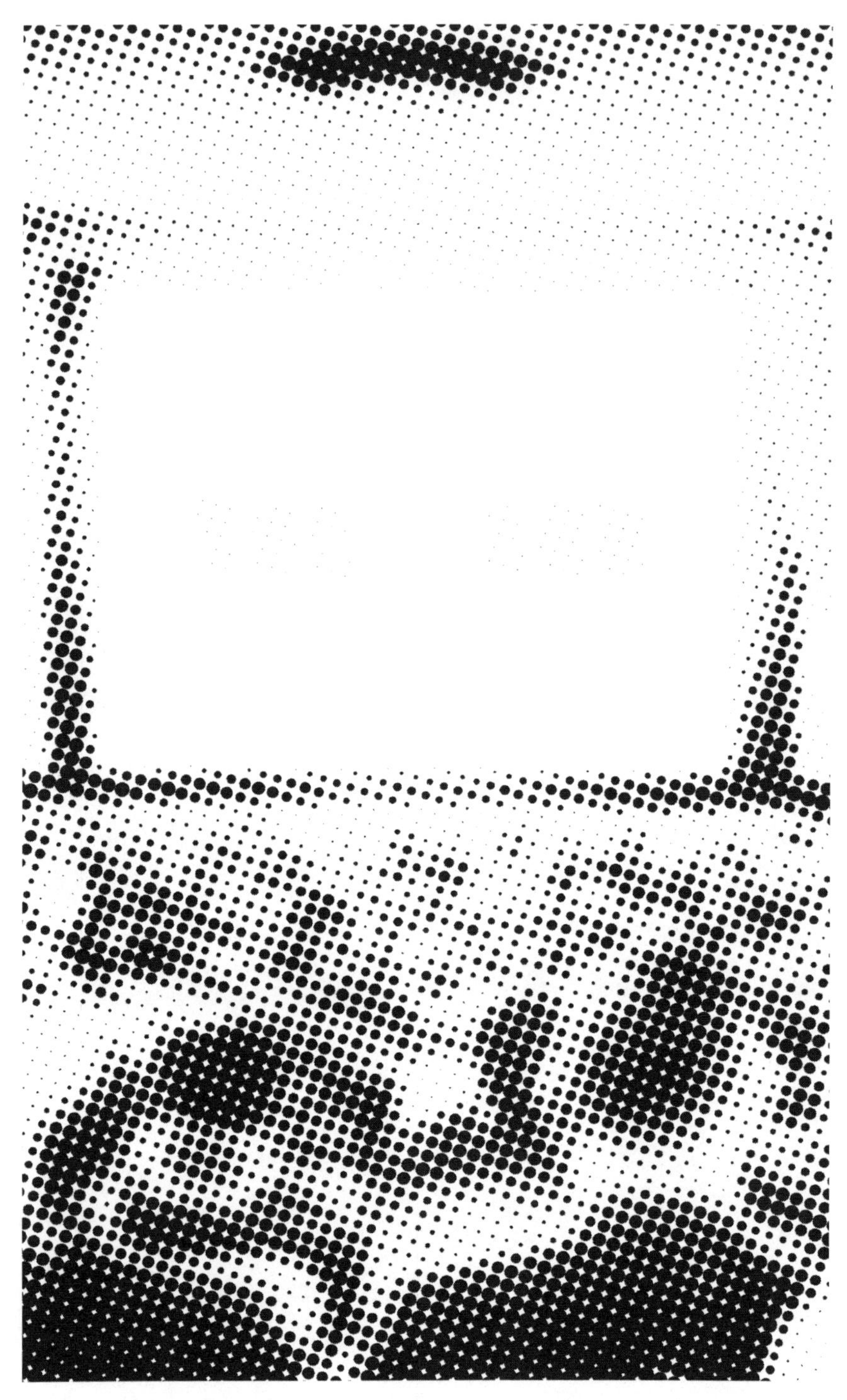

HOW TO FIND A REAL FILM INVESTOR

"The enemy of art is the absence of limitations."

—ORSON WELLES

One day I got a text message from a high-profile industry associate. He asked if I was available to meet for lunch so he could introduce me to a fund manager who was in town only for a few days. I asked a few questions but didn't have time to conduct any meaningful due diligence. I was sitting in L.A. traffic mowing through a list of calls, and I didn't have any plans for lunch, so I agreed to the meeting. After all, this was a high-profile industry professional inviting me. As a matter of practice, I usually like to know who I'm meeting and have an agenda beforehand, so I can do my best to vet them out ahead of the meeting, and so that I am well prepared. But I didn't do that this time.

When I arrived, I had no idea what to expect. It was tough to size up this alleged "fund manager." He wasn't wearing a watch, and he was dressed casually, which is typical for L.A.; in fact, they say the more dressed up you are in L.A., the less money you have. We began exchanging pleasantries, and I immediately noticed he was obnoxiously arrogant. This is always a sign of a talentless bullshitter, but I gave him the benefit of the doubt and tried not to judge him too soon. He picked my brain a little about my company and plans, and I was vague. He then boasted about his many holdings in media, technology, aerospace, energy, entertainment, fashion, and the list went on and on. At that point, I knew what I was smelling was the all-too-familiar stench of bullshit that I have been around so many times before. When the check came, he didn't even reach for his wallet, and my business associate grabbed the check before I could get to it. He insisted on buying lunch for all of us while Mr. Fund Manager sat back and cleaned the food out of his teeth with a toothpick.

Upon arriving back to my office, and with a simple web search, I discovered this guy was a complete waste of time. This story is a perfect example of how sometimes good people get fooled by someone else, and they believe what they are representing is right, and the vicious cycle spreads like a disease from one person to another, feeding off this insatiable dream of being in the film business.

An amusing end to this story: months later, I was hanging out in the marina and noticed a rundown pontoon boat floating down the canal, and it was obviously out of place amongst the high-end yachts that line this basin. As the pontoon boat got closer, I recognized none other than Mr. Big Time Fund Manager. He was sitting at the end of the boat throwing back a tall can of Budweiser, no private jets or satellites in sight. This story is not meant to be a criticism of pontoon boats or Budweiser, but it was hilarious to see this guy in all of his trailer park glory, stripped down to what he is. It was truly unbelievable to see with my own eyes, but after a few moments, I realized I was witnessing his true identity.

HOW TO SPOT A FAKE

I promise that in your search for real film investors, most of the people you run across who claim to be "in the business" will be full of shit. Let's get that out of the way right upfront. If you take a walk through what I call the "no-badge zone" in the lobby at the Loews Hotel in Santa Monica, during the American Film Market, you will see those who, for one reason or another, do not have the credentials to officially attend the film market. They hang out in the lobby, by the bar and in other areas with fancy suits and arm candy, usually an (over-the-hill) aspiring actress. Or the guy with the pencil mustache and greased hair, wearing a beret and smoking jacket. He has a day job as a waiter at a Greek restaurant on Ventura Boulevard, but calls himself a writer and actor on LinkedIn with no IMDB credits other than a short film in 1999. They can't buy a pass to a film market, yet we're supposed to believe these people have access to millions of dollars. They come in all varieties—the most common are the middlemen who claim to have film funds or access to investors, the big shots who claim to have a $20-million project with half the money "in the bank," and the guys who "just closed" a billion-dollar Chinese film fund. The list goes on and on and on. These characters are all on a race to the bottom, and they will take you down with them if you're not careful.

I have met many colorful characters in my Hollywood adventures, from crazy billionaires renting out the top floor of a Beverly Hills hotel, surrounded by escorts and drugs, to a famous race car driver who would get drunk and race his Ferraris up and down Sunset Blvd before jumping on his private jet to Vegas, to the 20-something with a trust fund, snorting lines of cocaine poolside at the Chateau Marmont. Sometimes the people you meet have money, but it's not the kind of money you want or need in your life. These people bring baggage with them that is not worth your time. Do not take money from these reckless people, or they will take you down. They are magnets for lawsuits and scandal, and they can ruin your entire career.

Keeping up with these characters can be exhausting, and the varieties of crazy people and stories you meet in this business are never-ending. This industry attracts people from all over the world who operate at the fringes of the industry and in some cases, the fringes of society. In the best-case scenario, they had a brush with some remotely notable project or person years ago, and they will milk that experience as long as they can, or they may be the nephew or niece of someone legitimate and assume that somehow qualifies them to waste your time. You will no doubt kiss a few toads along the way, but eventually, you will develop a pretty accurate bullshit detector and be able to sniff these people out.

However, for now, here's the most practical advice I can give you on how to identify real investors.

HOW TO IDENTIFY REAL INVESTORS

Investors are people who have money under their direct control. They may have a line of credit or a fund, but most of the time, it is their own money. They are doctors, lawyers, dentists, real estate investors, business owners, and many, many other things. These people generally are not out looking for investment opportunities, and are especially not wandering film markets without credentials.

There are different levels of investors, too. Generally speaking, a billionaire is not going to be that excited about investing in a lower-budget film as it is not worth their time. They would rather spend it on a weekend in Monaco. If they're going to invest in a movie, it would likely be at a much higher budget level. Investors with net worths in the high six figures or seven- to nine-figure range are a better fit for smaller indie films.

I find that real investors generally fall into three buckets:

1) The Ego Investor
This is generally a person with a relatively boring profession

who wants something to talk about at the country club or wants to see their name or company name on a big screen so they can invite all their friends to the premiere and add "movie producer" to their long list of accomplishments. The Ego Investor is also the person who may ask you to put their daughter, niece, girlfriend, boyfriend, or mistress in the film. They will also want a chair on set with their name on it, and will no doubt assert their authority during production.

2) The I-Have-Always-Dreamed-of-Making-Movies Investor
This person is particularly tricky because they may have the ego side and will also have a strong opinion on all creative aspects of the film. They may want the last word on the script, the cast, the director, and/or the edit, and you will spend all of your time balancing this investor's subjective opinions against what the director wants—unless you all agree on everything, which would be pretty cool, but highly unlikely. From personal experience, most of these investors do not understand the creative process and will make the process more difficult than it needs to be.

3) The Money Investor
This is by far my favorite type of investor, and the one with which I have had the most success. This investor cares only about the money and the deal. The higher the risk, the higher the reward. They are all business all the time. They generally

won't care about the creative elements as much as the people they are trusting with their money and those people's comfort level with the risk. They will want a fast turnaround and high returns, often requiring their money back within 12-18 months at 20%-30% or more per annum.

There are always exceptions to these rules, and you will meet hybrids of these three types. No two investors are the same. They all come with their own set of challenges. It is your job to lay your cards on the table, listen, observe, and learn while deciding if an investor is a fit for you and your project.

TAKE ACTION: COUNTERINTUITIVE TIPS TO KEEP IN MIND

A real investor wants to give you the money as badly as you want to receive it. I know you probably think I'm exaggerating, but I'm not. Investors love investing. They love putting their money to work. They love success, and if you can bring them that, you will have an investor for life.

Sometimes it's easier to raise seven-figure budgets than six-figure-and-below budgets. Why? The perceived risk on a low-budget film with no names is much higher than a seven-figure movie with bankable names. However, these are dangerous waters as the industry continues to change. You could be overvaluing the names in your film if you're basing it on historical sales data. Again, this might be the investor's perspective, and you need to be able to speak to their concerns directly.

If you are a first-time feature producer, I highly recommend you do not attempt to raise more than $50,000 unless you are partnering with an established producer. Before asking for $50,000, I recommend you make a $10,000 feature film and turn a profit so you can use it as a case study when you are ready for a more significant budget. It does not cost any more to make it look and sound great—family, friends, and credit cards will usually get you to an amount good enough to grind out a feature, and then you can graduate to a higher budget level. You will make it much easier on yourself in the long run by taking this approach. You don't want to spend the next 5-10 years chasing a fantasy. I've seen it happen many times, even to high-profile people in the industry. Whichever direction you choose, it will swallow you up and spit you out over and over again, and before you know it, years will pass and you might find yourself wandering the lobby at AFM wearing a beret and a smoking jacket.

Real investors invest in people, not ideas. Once you fully grasp this concept, you will understand that raising money is about finding qualified investors whom you connect with, and nothing else. It would help if you learned to be equally selective about who you take money from. Work only with investors who you want to be your business partners. Desperation always leads to bad decisions and bad decisions always leads to wasted time and regrets.

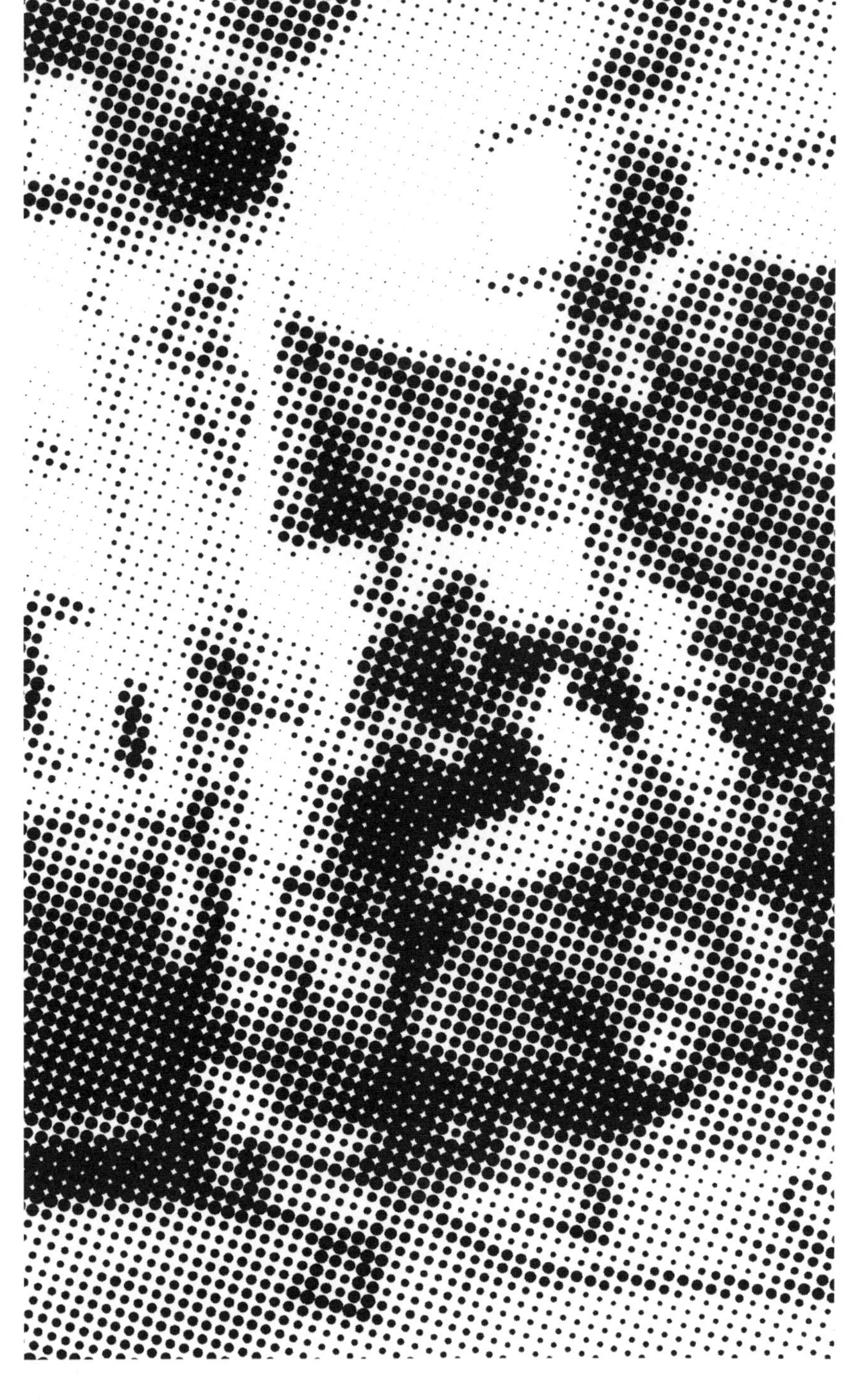

CHAPTER FIVE

WHO ARE YOU, AND WHAT DO YOU WANT?

"Evil breaks its chains and runs through the world like a mad dog. The poison affects us all. No one escapes."

—Ingmar Bergman

In one of my first real film pitch meetings years ago, a friend introduced me to an (Academy-Award-winning) investor/producer. After the very quick and painful pleasantries, I was relying on my friend to break the ice and set up the conversation, but I don't think he realized that, because instead, he politely asked for the restroom and then excused himself. Abandoned, I was all alone with the stone-faced investor, sitting opposite him in his large conference room overlooking downtown Beverly Hills. While I was scanning my brain for something witty to say, he was the first to break the silence: "Who are you, and what do you want?" This experience is perhaps one of the most important life lessons I've ever learned as a producer. Seems like the most straightforward question in the world, right? Under the circumstances, though, it was insanely difficult to answer clearly and concisely because I wasn't expecting that question, and it wasn't part of what I had ever imagined.

To avoid an embarrassing recurrence in any future meetings, I went home and prepared awesome PowerPoint decks with multiple full-color hard copies. I also had it available on my laptop, just in case an investor preferred I project it on a large screen while I walked around like Steve Jobs. I rehearsed it over and over again, and felt confident I would be ready to tackle any questions that would be thrown at me. The PowerPoint presentation worked great at informing those who could sit through it, but never really yielded the results I was looking for. Then one day, something happened that changed everything…

I was in Baton Rouge, Louisiana, for a meeting with a producer friend and one of his money people. This meeting was another great opportunity to use my PowerPoint deck in a real pitch. The investor's office was pretty far out of the city, in a small plantation town closer to the border of Mississippi. One gas station, one restaurant, and no cell service. My producer friend told me in advance that if we got more than 15-20 minutes, that meant the investor liked what he was hearing. And if the investor invited us to lunch, that meant he wanted what he was hearing.

So there I was, in the middle of nowhere, sitting with another stone-face real estate investor. He was a Money Investor and didn't care about anything else. I got halfway through slide two, and I was in the zone. Everything I rehearsed was coming out exactly as I planned, until the investor interrupted my magical moment and said, "Put that shit away, look me in the eyes, and tell me what you want."

It was then that I realized this was never going to be a dog-and-pony show like raising money in Silicon Valley or pitching a new ad campaign. I needed to get my head around another level of communication: deeper, more direct, less of a sales pitch and more of a personal conversation. I needed to be ready to put everything I had on the table, every time I met a new investor. This meeting was the moment I realized the power of being real, and, in many cases, raw: no sugar coating, no buzzwords, just straight talk. I decided to lay it all on the table, and not only did I get over 30 minutes in his office, he also invited us to lunch. And a few months later, I closed a sizeable deal with him. He remains one of my primary investor/partners to this day, and he will be for years to come.

GET COMFORTABLE WITH BEING UNCOMFORTABLE

Success never comes as a result of staying in your comfort zone. You must challenge yourself by taking actions that you may not have previously considered. You will never accomplish your goals by choosing the "safe" route. Whether it's a PowerPoint presentation or follow-up phone call, never be afraid to take action. I'm not talking about being a pushy salesperson. I'm talking about meaningful connections that make you stand out in the crowd. If you're not first, be different.

GIVE TO GET

The film industry is polluted with a culture of *takers*. These people always have their hand out, and they act as if the world owes them something. They don't believe in earning anything. Instead of giving and earning, they believe they are entitled to what it is they are seeking. Savvy businesspeople, investors or otherwise, will be looking to discover if you are a *taker* or a *giver*, whether they are conscious of it or not. Those who find success are almost always givers. It is essential to understand that establishing relationships with investors—or anyone else, for that matter—requires you to give first. If you enter into new conversations from a place of giving, you will see more people willing to give back. This can be challenging, and you will no doubt meet people who will discourage you from being a giver, but you must forge ahead and never let those bad experiences change who you are.

Never see a film pitch as taking anything. Always see it as earning a new relationship where you tell a person who you are, what you have, and what you need, and then hope they connect with you in a meaningful way. Make certain you are providing value in what you share with them—give them value first.

MAKE IT PERSONAL

Getting someone to invest in you is always about making a personal connection. Don't fake anything. Be genuine, and you will see the power of honesty work like magic. Whether they give you money or not, you will make a meaningful connection that will bring value in other ways—maybe a new mentor, or possibly a future investment. It never hurts to build your network of successful people.

PLAY THE LONG GAME

Take deep breaths, slow down, and take your time. When meeting an investor for the first time, or before they have expressed a genuine interest in investing in you, keep a long-game frame of mind. You should never rush or pass any of your pressure on an investor, or you will lose them early in the conversation. Developing relationships is like building a garden. You start by laying the right soil, carefully planting the right seeds, and then nurturing and caring for your garden over long periods before it grows. Meaningful relationships take time to develop, and some investors need more time than others to get comfortable with you. They want to see consistency and unwavering dedication, and sometimes these relationships take months or even years to develop. Do not place arbitrary deadlines on yourself, or your eagerness may be interpreted as desperation. Be focused and take action, but slow down and think long term. If for some reason they don't invest in your current film, you will have time to nurture the relationship for your next movie, or the one after that.

BE A PRODUCER FIRST

Too many people in the independent film business are trying to be too many things. You can be a writer, a director, an actor, or even all of the above, but you should always be a producer FIRST and before any other role. Investors look at the producer as the grown-up and CEO in charge of the show. They want to know that the person looking in their eyes and introducing this project to them is also the person who will be responsible for being a good steward of their money. Producers should never be emotionally attached to any of the creative elements of the project; in fact, they should be emotionally *detached*, especially while raising money. Most of the time, investors DO NOT want to be looking in the eyes of a writer, a director, or an actor who is drunk with emotion for their passion project that they believe will change the world. That meeting may or may not come in the future, if and when the investor is ever interested in continuing the conversation with you.

It is essential to note that being a writer, director, actor, or any other role DOES NOT automatically qualify you to be a producer. Be honest with yourself. Know what you're good at, and surround yourself with people who are better than you at what they are there to do. Most self-made investors are successful in part because they are "street smart." They may have impressive college degrees, but their success stories almost always involve developing razor-sharp survival skills by finding their paths to raise money and building their empires from the ground up. I cannot stress this enough: never, ever bullshit an investor, or your deal is dead. You cannot pretend to be someone you're not. Street-smart investors will see right through you. Remember, investors invest in people. If you wonder how so many terrible movies are made every year, there is likely a dynamic producer involved in each of those projects who was able to raise the financing. And I should mention, many of those bad movies recoup their investments.

I can't stress this enough: if you are not ready and able to be a producer 100% and lay everything on the table, you should not be speaking with investors. You need to be an ambassador of the project you are representing. You need to know every detail, inside out and forward and backward. Be ready to present the plan in 25 or 1000 words. It would be best if you NEVER were a writer, a director, or an actor when presenting to an investor. Making a movie is like going to war, and as the producer, you are the general of your army. As the general, you have the responsibility not only of building your army, but also of assigning your inner circle of captains and developing a battle strategy. You're aiming for the best execution of the finished film, on time and budget, while also identifying the risks to the best of your ability. You must be ready, willing, and able to carry that torch from start to finish, and nothing can stop you. You must be pragmatic and able to see the "worst case" in every scenario with razor-sharp precision.

PAY ATTENTION

In today's world of independent film production, we are forced to wear many hats. The need to serve different roles is equally good and bad. The good news is that we understand what it takes to make a movie from start to finish. The bad news is that we understand what it takes to make a movie from start to finish. Own it, be the CEO of your film, and don't let anything stand in your way.

A producer might serve in multiple roles once the film is financed and ready to go. You may have written the script, you may be planning to direct, and you may expect to be an actor in the film. By no means am I suggesting you conceal this information from the investor, but I am suggesting you keep any other role on the back burner. Most of the time, those roles are useless when asking for money from real investors. I will caution you that unless you have an actual and established track record of bringing measurable value, introducing another role at any point will likely muddy the waters in your investor pitch, and in some cases turn him or her off completely. That's why it is best to keep the producer role completely separate from the other roles as much as possible. This strategy will work to your advantage.

Visualize it this way: as a producer, your goal is to work your way to the investor's side of the desk. You are on their team, and it is now you and them against the world. It is more difficult to do that when you add on other roles, especially if you're not a well established writer, director, or actor who brings real and measurable value, as a real commodity.

HAVE A WELL-DEVELOPED PERSONAL BRAND

I'm not talking about a logo or a clever name for your production company. I'm talking about your brand. Be true to yourself, be 100% honest, and embrace your strengths and weaknesses, and everything else will fall into place. Half the world will connect with you, and the other half will not. That's it; it's that simple. Begin building your brand with your values and principles (trustworthy, honest, direct, etc.), then your beliefs (I am motivated by...), then your reputation (I'm known for...), then your behavior (my personality is...), then your skills (I excel at...), and finally your image (my style is...). These attributes should be communicated organically through honest and direct communication with the investor. Remember, this is not their first rodeo, and you will never fool them. Honesty is the most powerful communication tool you have, especially with seasoned investors who likely tango with the best.

BUILD YOUR TEAM

Fight, flight, or mate: there are only three kinds of people in the world. Are you a fighter? Do you run from conflict? Or do you make friends? It's critical to understand this when building a team and understanding how investors will see you. If you are a fighter, you will need a friend-maker on your side. If you are a friend-maker, you will need a fighter on your team, and if you are a runner, you need both a fighter and friend-maker. Develop your team to be your inner circle, and get to the point where you can include them in your investor and other related meetings. Think of film production as going to war, where every day is a new battle. Out of the three kinds of people, who do you want in the foxhole with you? Who do you think an investor will want in charge of their money? Be honest with yourself, and it will only help to accomplish your goals. DO NOT pretend to be any of these things, or you will likely never get the money.

PARK GREED AND EGO

Generally speaking, two things kill business more than anything else: greed and ego. When I was in the advertising world, I was surrounded by people I thought were difficult and complex. There are layers of corporate egos mixed with frustratingly subjective opinions that constantly clashed, and months of grinding you down until you are so worn out that you don't care. That was a walk in the park compared to the film business.

The two things that kill business, in general, are ironically the two things that are most prominent in the film business. If you have an ego problem, please, do us both a favor and park that shit at the door before you meet with any investor. A big ego is the kiss of death with street-smart investors. A big ego does not communicate with confidence. It conveys weakness, problems, and conflict that lead to bad decisions. When you are 100% honest and open, it is easy to be confident in what you know and what you don't know. Big egos are usually cover-ups for talentless people who are not satisfied in their abilities. Real investors know this and can spot it a mile away.

HAVE SKIN IN THE GAME

Investors want producers to have skin in the game. This doesn't mean they want to hear about your film's "years or months of development." That's a black hole vacuum of pretend time that happened before the investor's involvement, and it carries ZERO value. They don't give one shit about what you did before their participation, how many lunches you bought the writer, or how many other investors you took out to an expensive dinner. Know how much, in actual money, you have already invested into real documented development, and into hiring writers, producers, or other service providers. How can you expect an investor to believe in you and your project if you don't believe in yourself enough to put in your own money first?

Investors hate seeing ridiculous producer fees or any inflated above-the-line fees. Be realistic and practical when proposing your fees. Have a logical explanation (example: $2000 per week for 8-12 weeks). Investors hate ambiguous numbers that make them feel like you're one of the people on the opposite side of the desk. Any indication of a big ego and any perception of greed on your part will kill the deal instantly in the investor's mind, and it will be impossible for you to change their opinion once that seed has been planted. It will only grow more significant, and eventually, the deal will fall apart.

DON'T MENTION YOUR FRIENDS

There is no place for "friends" in private investment financing. Don't call anyone on this project a "friend." Generally speaking, this is an overused term in the film world and a word that street-smart investors do not value or like. It usually means you are either too close to a person to see if they bring value to the project, or that you are too stupid to know when someone is taking advantage of you. Either way, it is terrible news for you and another kiss of death. Do not involve your spouse, your girlfriend or boyfriend, or any other personal connection for the same reasons—unless they happen to be your producing partner, which I have seen before. It is acceptable and encouraged (when the time is right) to mention you have tried-and-true crew members who have proven to be loyal, reliable, and good at what they do.

PREPARE YOUR ELEVATOR SPEECH

As I mentioned before, have the 25-word pitch on the tip of your tongue at all times. This will be the thing you say over and over again when people ask you about your project. You should have the general version and the investor version loaded and ready to go at any time. If you are first honest with yourself about who you are, what you have, and what you want, and you embrace your strengths and weaknesses, you will be prepared for any question that comes at you from anyone at any time.

BE HONEST ABOUT WHAT YOU CAN DELIVER

Do not misrepresent your cast or overvalue yourself or your team. Do not include big names in your pitch if you are at all unsure about whether you can deliver. If you are planning a larger budget film ($1M and above), consider attaching a casting director early and have your "sweet spot" budget level with a few realistic names. Remember that we are all commodities, so a savvy film investor may ask for bigger names, which will require more money, a more prominent producer, and more significant director. Do not leave this part of the equation open for discussion, as this is always a moving target. If the investor is the right fit and the project has a realistic sweet spot, you should be able to defend your casting choices logically.

BE REALISTIC ABOUT YOUR BUDGET

I cannot remember how many times people have come to me and said, "I have a $3-million movie." Then they'll pitch the film and proposed cast, and when I tell them it sounds more like a $1-million movie, they'll respond, "We can make it for that…" That is instant death for a producer, because it's a dead giveaway that you don't have command of your project.

There is a tribe in Africa that makes jewelry and sells it on the street. An African billionaire once told me that if you walk up to one of these vendors and ask for the price of an item, they will answer, "How much do you want to pay?" This practice has earned them a reputation for being untrustworthy. If they were to just name a price, they would be better off than changing the amount every time they talk to a new person. Once you've established a valid budget range, do not be overly flexible with your budget. If you follow my advice and have good sound thinking and planning behind your project, no one can question your decisions. Don't just pull a number out of your ass. Investors will know, or they will eventually figure it out.

Do not build your budget on a "died and went to indie film production heaven" mindset. Instead, think about the very bare bones of your physical production. You may not be able to rent a drone and hire an operator, or you may have to lose the crane shot in downtown, or you might not be able to shut down a public street or rent a rain machine. Think about what the real and practical number is, with everyone being paid fairly and without asking for any special favors from anyone. If you're fortunate enough to get your film financed, you can go back and negotiate, ask for favors, and save money on other items so you can add in things like a crane shot or a second camera assistant. Most of the time, those creative elements will not make you any more money, so it is a fine line to walk, and it's up to you to keep that barrier as low as possible. Your number-one goal after completing the film will be to recoup the investment as fast as you can. This should be your only measure of success at this stage.

Treat your script the same way: strip it down to bare story points, and keep it streamlined and practical without compromising the quality of the execution. Do not overschedule yourself. Give yourself time to get the coverage you need to cut together a great film. A great, streamlined film will be more successful than a mediocre movie with more bells and whistles. Keep it simple and easy to understand, especially if this is your first film at this budget level.

A good producer knows their market, keeps up with industry data, monitors their proposed cast's past films and how they are performing, keeps up with what major distributors are acquiring from independent film markets, and watches trends in genres and talent. Don't get lost in the emotions of your project. Not everyone will like or understand it the way you do. Be realistic about your goals. Slow and steady is the name of the game.

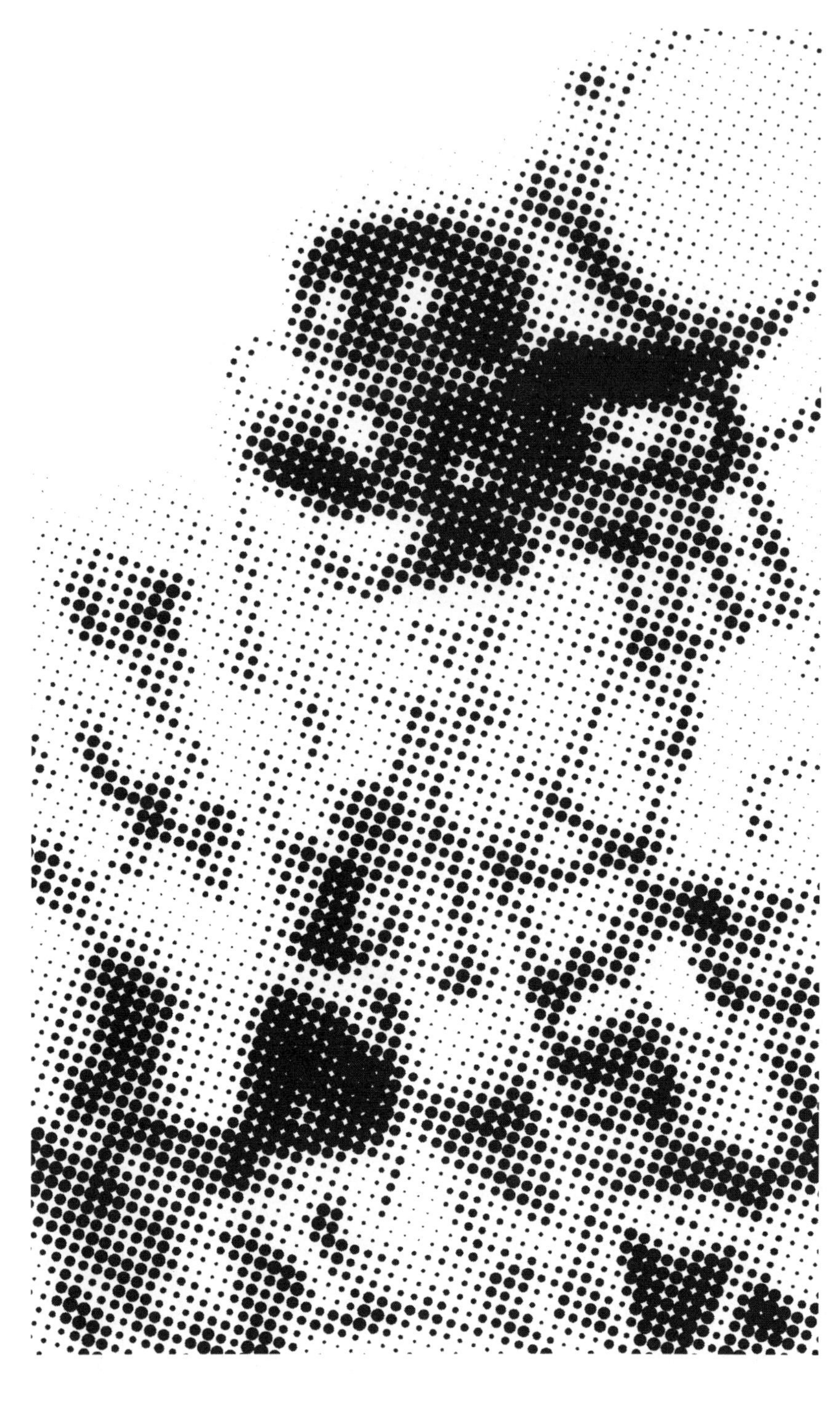

CHAPTER SIX

INSIDE THE MIND OF A FILM INVESTOR

"Nothing recedes like success."

—Bryan Forbes

One day, a producer and business associate of mine asked if he could take a meeting in our conference room. We had nothing scheduled that afternoon, so I agreed to let him use it. He and his team were to pitch an investor on a new film project. He arrived early and asked if he could share his pitch with me and get my feedback. I listened to the whole thing and gave him some quick advice. Above all, I told him to make it more about the deal and less about the script. He didn't seem to understand what I meant and looked a little confused. The investor arrived, and I knew he was legit the moment I saw him. The producers introduced us, we exchanged a few pleasantries, and he even complimented my office before they all went into the conference room for their meeting, which had nothing to do with me or my company.

About ten minutes into the meeting, my assistant came to my office door and said, "The investor is asking for you in the conference room." I was curious what was going on, so I got up, walked down the hall and entered the silent room to blank stares as all of us were trying to figure out why he had requested to see me. Without delay and before I could even take a seat, the investor looked straight in my eyes from across the room and asked, "Would you invest your money in this project?"

This short meeting was one of those situations that separates me as a businessman, and I had to be honest as I was representing myself, my company, and those who have trusted me with their money. I looked him in the eyes and said, "No, not as it has been presented to me today." As the others in the room all looked disappointed and no doubt hated the fact that I had said that, the investor slowly cracked a grin with intense satisfaction and almost relief in his eyes that he had connected with one of us in a meaningful way. One word was all it took to establish trust. These producers would have been better off taking my idea: focus more on the deal, less on the script. Instead, they were drunk with passion and had not adequately planned or communicated the business side of their project.

You cannot compromise your integrity, and you must treat an investor's money as if it is your own. Take it personally—what would you do if that money was coming out of your bank account? How different would you want that deal to be? How much would you care about the script if you were not a filmmaker? These are all things you need to sort out before ever pitching anything to anyone.

There's always a reason an investor will take a meeting. It might be an obligation through a mutual or personal connection, or maybe they are interested for a very specific reason. Objective number one: find the investor's "pain"—why are they speaking with you? Do they want money? Recognition? Friends? Maybe good photo ops for Facebook or Instagram? Perhaps something to add to their legacy? Find that out as quickly as possible. Do not promise them huge returns on their investment; you can't control the market. Focus only on things you can control, like doing your best to cover the investment by producing the best film possible. The investor's first concern will be preserving their capital, and that's precisely what you should address before anything else.

A real investor wants to know who you are, what you've done (in and out of the film business), and what qualifies you to produce this film, not necessarily exclusive to the film business. It is less about the dollar amount and more about the risk. As I mentioned earlier, smaller film budgets are often more challenging than larger budgets with more significant name talent because of the perceived risk. Real investors generally do not boast about all the money they have—this is usually the clear sign of a bullshitter, a waste of your time, a talentless egomaniac, or worse, all of the above.

Money has a different meaning to the investor than it does to you. Where you see a $3 cup of coffee, they might see how much they had to earn (gross) plus sales tax, and that cup may cost over $6 in their minds. This is why some investors seem "cheap"—they simply don't see the value in paying $6 for a cup of coffee. Your perspective of money is likely a destination, or a means to an end. It is all you need to make your film a reality; it will get you to the finish line, put you on the map, and build your career. Real investors don't give one shit about any of those things. To an investor, money is nothing more than a tool. It flows like water, and their game is to find ways to grow their capital by utilizing, among other things, money. They leverage time, risk, and even debt with return on investment. If their stock portfolio is earning them an average of 7% a year, with relatively lower risk than a film, why would they want to move any money into film production? The answer could be the chance of significantly more returns over the same period, or that they see other personal and professional rewards.

THERE ARE TYPICALLY TWO TYPES OF INVESTMENTS IN FILM:

1) **Debt:** Debt is usually utilized to finance a portion of the production that will be covered within 12-18 months of taking the funds. Essentially, a debt investment is a loan. Examples of debt investments can be advances on rebates and other incentives or other financing that you may not be able to access until after the film is complete. Debt investors usually do not get any equity or percentage of ownership in the film.

2) **Equity:** The standard equation in a film deal structure is that equity investors get their principal investment plus a 20% premium in first position (after debt, deferments, and fees) plus 50% equity (ownership), which entitles them to 50% of the

producer's net profits after recouping the capital and the premium. 20% sounds great if you can get it back to them within 12-24 months, but in this example, anything beyond that will start to get close to the same returns as what their stock portfolio is earning without the same level of risk.

The reality is that you will likely not recoup an equity investment in 12-24 months unless you have pre-sales or another distribution deal in place, which we are not talking about in this book. That's why you need to find their "pain" and figure out what their biggest motivation is to consider investing in your film. Ironically, the best way to address risk in this business is for an investor to spread their investment in multiple films, and statistically, at least one of the movies will do better than the rest in the slate, but we'll focus on one for now.

Think of how rapidly the value of money, inflation, and the perception of money is changing, even since the mid-90s. Remember the film *Pulp Fiction*, when Vincent Vega says, "I gotta know what a $5 shake tastes like…"? In today's world, $5 is a typical or even reasonable price for a shake, but in 1994, it was considered extravagant enough to mention in the context of this scene. What will that shake cost in two more decades? In recent years, the rate of inflation has gone from a high of around 4% to as low as 1%. When you factor that into your equation, it reduces the investor's bottom line even more, especially when you compound year after year. Investors think about growing their money beyond inflation so that if and when they ever retire, they will have enough income and assets for themselves, their children, and future generations. What good does it do to have millions of dollars sitting in the bank without growth? Because of inflation, that money will shrink by 1% to 4% per year or more.

Wealthy people's portfolios will often include real estate, annuities, stocks, bonds, and many others. The idea of investing outside standard investment vehicles can be exciting to an investor. You're not asking for money for a start-up that may or may not ever get off the ground; rather, you're asking for money for a product that you will create in a specific window of time. There is a high worldwide demand for this product, and you will deliver it come hell or high water. The reality of supply and demand should be at the core of your financial pitch to equity investors.

The film business thrived during the Great Depression because audiences enjoyed escaping reality and living vicariously in the worlds that filmmakers created. Content is available to everyone in today's world, and it lives on every device. A movie is an asset that generates revenue, yet it requires almost no maintenance once it's completed—no plumbers, no roofing, no property taxes, and little of anything else. In today's market, you might sell worldwide rights to the film and make all your money upfront, or you might distribute on a territory-by-territory and rights basis and enjoy the income over many years. It is essential to make sure that your target isn't just a 20% premium, but multiple streams of income above and beyond that for years to come.

When Warren Buffet talks about investing in gold, he makes the distinction between productive and non-productive assets. If you own an ounce of gold today, you can hold it for the next 30 years. You can touch it, polish, and stare at it, and at the end of 30 years, you will still have an ounce of gold. Buffet compares it to 100 acres of farmland that will produce income over that time, and at the end of 30 years, you still have a productive asset that will historically appreciate above the rate of inflation. A film can be a productive asset, depending on your distribution strategy. It can make you multiple streams of income for 20+ years, or you may choose to accept potentially less money upfront (still turning a profit) if given the opportunity to sell the film outright.

Like a film, the stock market comes with inherent risk and an average 7% to 10% returns per year for most savvy long-term investors. They can earn cash income or compound their earnings over time. If your investor trusts you to deliver a quality product and recoup their capital, you will have an investor for life. The upside to a film can be vast: some $3-million to $5-million films are making $25 million or more, and there are $100,000 films making $250K and up. Those are great returns for anyone. If an investor spreads their investments over several film projects, historically their returns will likely outperform stock holdings in shorter-term investments. However, that has everything to do with the quality of the production and your distribution strategy, which we are not covering in this book. It's important to note that statistically, most of those films will lose money or take 3-5 or more years to recoup the investment.

When looking for new investors, do not go to the same wells as everyone else, as you will likely find them empty. Most private film investors are not in the film business. You will have much more success finding independently wealthy individuals who are outside the industry and willing to invest in film. It is your job to lay out your plan to them. Always start with the deal, and hope the investor connects with you and your project. Remember, build and lead with your business strategy first, and consider all the other investment options that person has available to them. Your idea is not that special. Make it about the deal, and represent yourself honestly and openly. Be the captain of your ship, and spend the time to educate your investor with a mindset of giving first.

CHAPTER SEVEN

THE "VEGAS" NUMBER

"Art depends on luck and talent."

—Francis Ford Coppola

There is an interesting phenomenon called crowdfunding that has surfaced in recent years. Sites like Kickstarter and GoFundMe have brought out a charitable side in all of us. What is particularly interesting is that people are willing to donate to filmmakers with little to nothing in personal return. I have a theory that every one of us has a number—a dollar amount that we could throw on the table and not be hurt if we lost it. It might be $20, $500, or even $100,000. I call this the "Vegas" number. It is an amount that you will give away for the right reason, or for no reason at all.

I have met filmmakers who have raised money by contacting business owners, doctors, friends, and family. Maybe it's a $50,000 budget, and you get 50 people to give you $1000 in exchange for credit and a possible 20% premium on their money. Maybe you get 100 people to give $500, or any combination. I don't care if it is $20 or $1000—virtually every single person you know or can access with a little effort will have a Vegas number. If you consider the time it takes to develop relationships with investors at hundreds of thousands or millions of dollars, the Vegas number investor may be a better target, especially if your film is a micro-budget project. You'll be amazed how much perceived value there is for someone to have their name listed on a movie as an executive producer on IMDB.

Imagine you are a dentist or chiropractor at a dinner party or country club. There is nothing sexy about cavities, gum disease, or spinal alignment. You're giving these people something they don't have: a sexy title. Now, these dentists and doctors can say, "I'm a film producer," and you'll be amazed how people respond to just this alone. You could offer tiers of investments, and one of the levels could even include onscreen credit for their business or practice.

Be creative about making contact with new people; find an exciting way to get their attention. A simple phone call or email might not be good enough. Instead, try a personal letter introducing yourself, and then follow up with a call. How many people write letters today? Maybe you can include a flash drive with your reel or short film and a video clip with a personal introduction to you and your team? Find a way to show your creativity in the way you communicate; showing is always better than telling.

Remember, you are not asking for donations like some of these crowdfunding websites. You're asking for equity investments in your film with a 20% premium. Be honest with them about what you're doing, tell the Vegas number investor that you would prefer to piece together your project, be frugal and responsible, and give them frequent updates on the status of your production.

I know this sounds like a lot of work, but I guarantee you will finance your film. The time it will take is entirely up to you. There are no excuses not to make this work. If you are a first-time filmmaker, I highly recommend you make a high-quality short film with the tools you have available to you today, even if those tools are an iPhone and a couple of friends. No excuses. Vegas number investors may want to see pretty pictures, and you need something to show.

Utilizing the Vegas number strategy, you should make the best film possible for the least amount of money. Your intent is to build a great case study: a well executed film that recoups the investment and turns a profit.

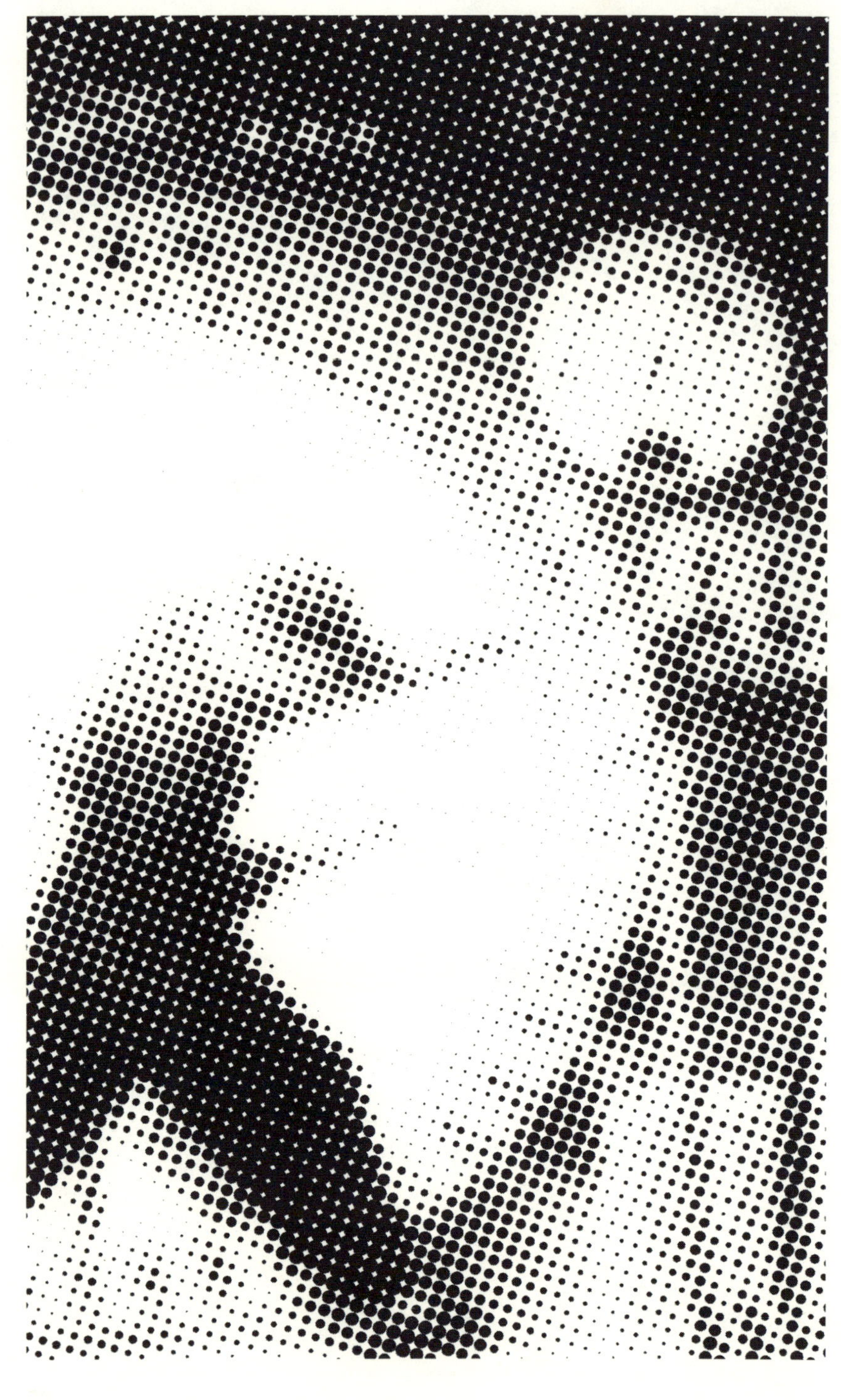

CHAPTER EIGHT

WHY? ART, BUSINESS, EGO

"The beautiful is hidden from the eyes of those who are not searching for the truth…"

—Andrei Tarkovsky

Why are you making movies? Is it art? The business? Your ego? Be honest with yourself, and form that part of your brand. Real investors will look for your essence, and they want to know what motivates you. It's OK to enjoy the showman side that feeds your ego, it's OK to do it for the love of the art, and it's OK to love the business side. It's *not* OK to try and fake any of these motivations. The more open you are, the more you will connect with everyone, not just investors. The power is in being passionate and honest with yourself, first. Find your WHY.

As an investor, I once made the mistake of trusting in someone who misrepresented themselves to me. I didn't take the time to understand their WHY. I learned the hard way what it means to have an irresponsible and untalented child at the helm of a film. It was painful and very costly, and what I discovered is that most seasoned film investors know what to look for. At that time, I had not yet learned the importance of this lesson. If you bought this book and you're reading it, chances are you are serious about being a producer and getting your films financed. If, for some reason, you are in this game to turn your production into a party for you and your friends and squander the opportunity, you will only burn bridges for yourself, and it will eventually catch up to you in a big way.

At the time of finishing this book, I was offered a lead producer role on a new project that was to be helmed by a first-time director and writer who had teed up private investors (family and friends) for a seven-figure budget. There were red flags with this first-time filmmaker as I was still searching for his WHY. I couldn't figure out why he made me uncomfortable, but I agreed to meet his investors, who were in from out of town. Maybe meeting them would help me figure this guy out. When I met the investors for the first time and looked in their eyes, I promised if my company and I agreed to take this film on that I, as producer, would do everything in my power to make the best film possible to protect their investment. They were solid and they made me comfortable enough to continue the conversation. I went on to recommend against a movie at this budget level for a first-time director, and I explained to them that to properly cast the film, we would need an excellent screenplay. After reading the first draft of the script, I realized it required a lot of work, and learned that a couple actors had passed on the roles before my involvement. I gave constructive feedback, but I was treading lightly because I knew the writer had a fragile ego. He had worked as an assistant on a film set 15 years ago and had functioned as an executive producer on a few small reality shows with no other real industry experience. The casting was going to be tough.

We got through one round of script development and then a second before I realized this first-time writer had hit a wall—he didn't even understand how to apply the feedback to the script. I suggested several times through the process that we bring in another writer to help, but he wouldn't have it. Eventually, his ego got the best of him, and he couldn't handle me pushing for a better script, so he stopped taking my calls and shifted on me like Dr. Jekyll and Mr. Hyde. He was angry, defensive, and went as far as lying in an attempt to make me look bad to his investors. I had overlooked red flags that I would typically never ignore because I had connected with his investors and believed they would give me the authority to carry out my responsibilities as producer. Thankfully, it was early enough in the process, and we had not taken the project around town, so I had a long conversation with one of the investors to explain my position, then bowed out of the project before any real damage had been done. Life is too short, and I've worked too hard to deal with erratic people at this level. Fragile egos drive people to desperation when they are challenged and forced to look at themselves. A truly talented person would be confident in their abilities and open to collaboration, especially as a first-time filmmaker.

Even more concerning, I had planned to bring a six-figure investment to this film myself and to utilize my network to get the best cast possible. I had not spent enough time understanding the director's WHY. What I realize now is that this project was nothing more than a feeble attempt for the director to legitimize himself. He was driven by ego, and his desire to not share the spotlight with anyone had become more of a priority to him than the need to make a great film.

Having a clear understanding of your WHY is critical to connecting with real investors. The WHY is more important than the WHAT and the HOW. The WHY will give you your mantra, like Apple computers' "to change the world." What is your mantra? Why are you in this business? What is your motivation? Your endgame? Believe it or not, this is very important, and even though an investor may not ask the question directly, they are unconsciously looking for that answer.

The WHY tells investors what you're all about, what kind of person you are, and how you think. If you start with the WHY, everything else is easy to drive home. The great filmmaker Garry Marshall said, "I like to make people laugh." As simple as this is, it is insanely powerful and defines who Garry was as a human being. His smile and his words take on more meaning now that we understand where he's coming from and what he was trying to accomplish.

Stanley Kubrick might have wanted to give us a genuine connection to truth through film when he said, "The most terrifying fact about the universe is not that it is hostile but that it is indifferent; but if we can come to terms with this indifference and accept the challenges of life within the boundaries of death—however mutable man may be able to make them— our existence as a species can have genuine meaning and fulfillment. However vast the darkness, we must supply our own light." Fritz Lang might have been wanting to share compassion with the world through his films when he said, "There can be no understanding between the hand and the brain unless the heart acts as mediator." Every great artist or businessperson understands the WHY and lives by it.

RESISTANCE

Not coming to terms with your WHY will cause resistance that will eventually create barriers between you and your goals. Some resistance can be easily understood, like bad weather or working with the wrong people. Be honest with yourself first. Why are you making movies? Why do you want to be a producer? Do not attempt to conceal this from anyone. No one in the world can overcome these barriers for you; this is something that took me a long time to fully understand. The other part that was very difficult for me was accepting that most of the resistance we all experience is brought on by our own actions, or, in some cases, lack thereof. Coming to terms with your WHY is the ultimate acceptance of responsibility and accountability that will lead to overcoming these barriers, and there is no other path to success. Everyone, but most importantly investors, will appreciate a hero's journey, and every one of us has a story to share. The essence of our WHY is rooted in this journey. The stories I share with you in this book about my own journey are meant to help you understand where I've been and where I am coming from and better understand my WHY.

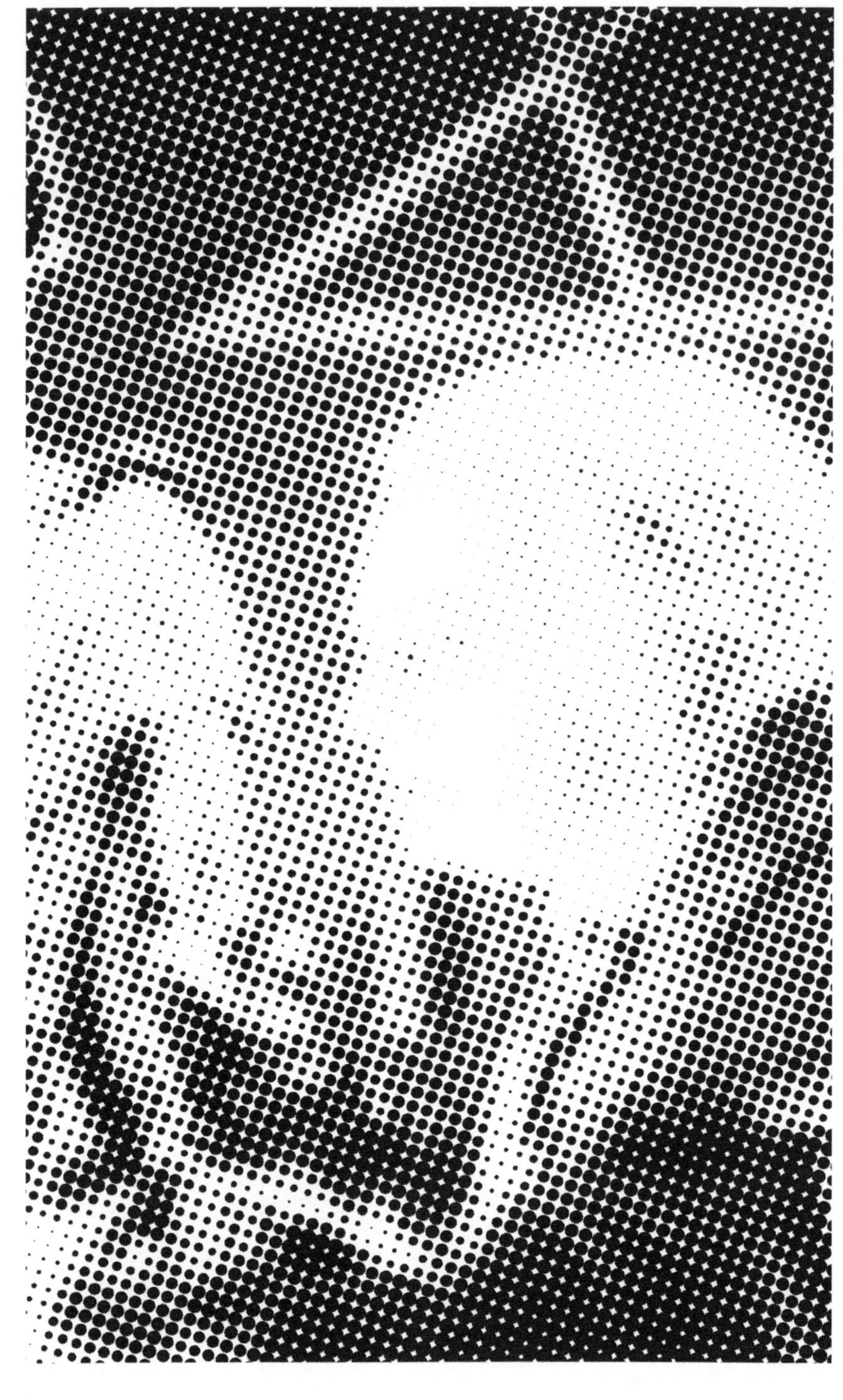

CHAPTER NINE

FILL YOUR "TOOLBOX"

*"All I need to make a comedy is a park,
a policeman and a pretty girl."*

—CHARLIE CHAPLIN

I have this simple but effective analogy that I use with my kids and other young people who have asked for advice. In life, we have a toolbox full of essential stuff. The tools in our toolbox can make life easier and accelerate our success. Conversely, a lack of tools can slow us down in many ways. I believe one of the most important tools you can have in your toolbox is a college degree. You don't have to be a film school grad to be a successful filmmaker. I would even say that a business degree will work much harder for you when it comes to raising money, making deals, and understanding marketing and monetization at a deeper level, but any skills—whether creative, technical or business—can be learned at any time. For the sake of this message, I will stress that any college degree in your toolbox will help you in life.

Other examples of essential tools are money and credit. Having an excellent credit rating will allow you to access lower-interest financing and credit cards, and may even help you land a job. Technical training and certificates are excellent. So are trade associations and memberships to institutions that give you a platform for networking and developing business opportunities.

Build a strong network by developing strategic alliances with service providers, crew, other producers, distributors, and, of course, potential investors. A good producer maintains a strong pool of talented and likeminded people in their toolbox. Remember, give first and others will reciprocate. Attend film festivals and film markets whenever possible, and network with everyone you can. Meet with college placement offices. Take meetings with service providers, like post-production companies, attorneys, accountants, and camera and gear rental companies. Form an alliance by asking what you and your team can do to help them provide the best service possible for your production. Take the time to develop key relationships, and you will build a solid network of people who will care about delivering for you on time and on budget. I'm not suggesting this activity replace your search for investors, but you never know: you may end up indirectly stumbling onto a potential investor or service provider willing to defer fees. Passion is contagious.

It is never too late to build your toolbox. The more tools you have, the stronger your foundation can be. Remember, it all takes action. Your phone will not ring, the email or text will not come in. You will likely not be an Instagram or YouTube star, so stop thinking like an amateur, grow up, dust off your toolbox, and start filling it with tools. Community colleges, trade programs, and now even camera and gear stores have masterclasses and workshops. There are countless resources online for technical training and many excellent books available on any subject. With the excess of information available to us today, there is no excuse for not educating yourself. Learning is as important as earning a living or caring for your physical health.

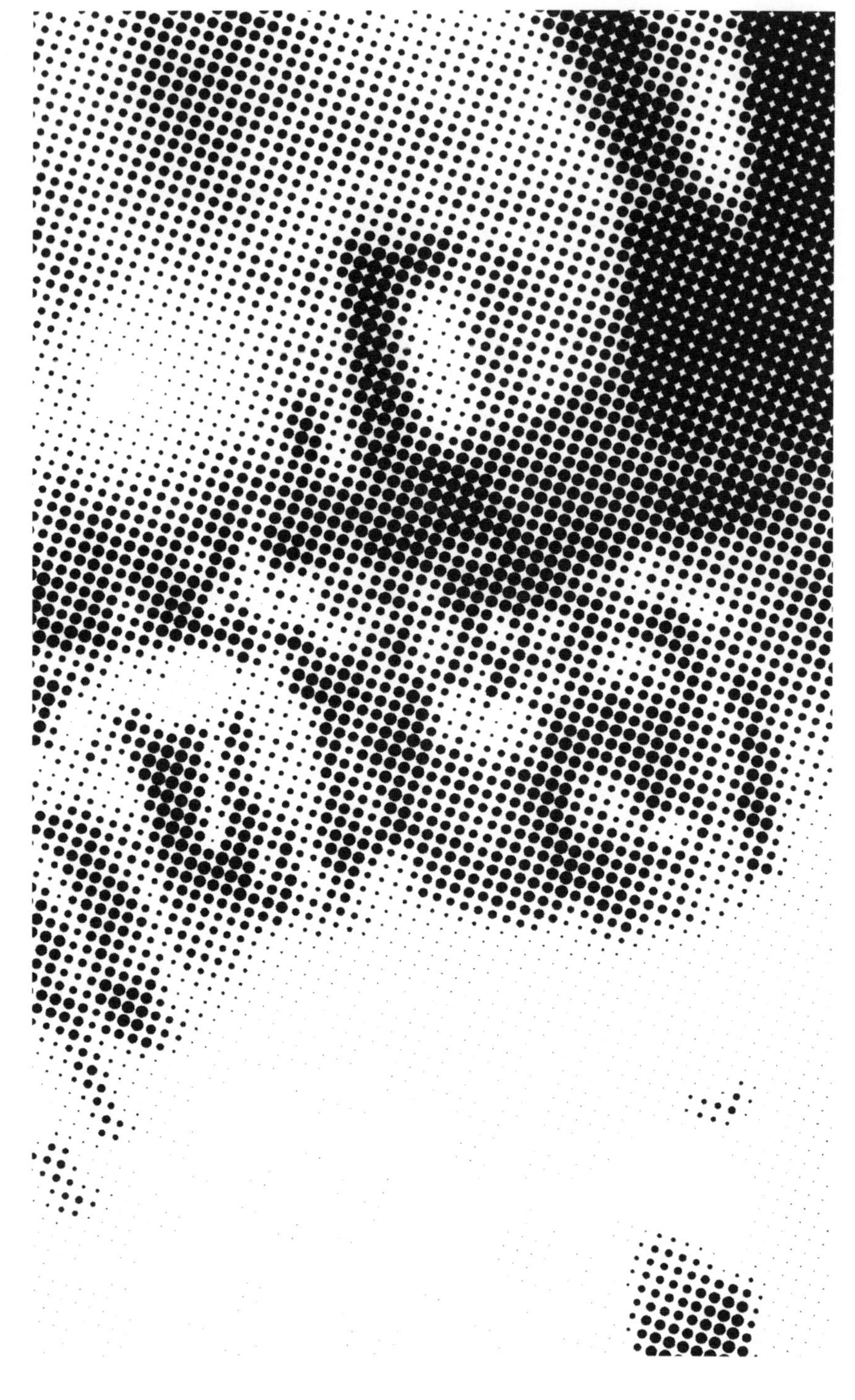

CHAPTER TEN

MASTER YOUR CRAFT

"I can't think how anyone can become a director without learning the craft of cinematography."

—Gus Van Sant

This is an incredibly important concept to truly understand. To add to its complicated nature, mastering your craft contradicts the industry "standards" that we have all been conditioned to believe. Early filmmakers like Auguste and Louis Lumière made movies piece by piece, with small casts and crews. They rolled up their sleeves and worked on every aspect of their films. The legendary Georges Méliès was known for directing, writing, acting, special effects, camera work, editing, music, and the list goes on and on. The filmmakers of the past had to be masters of almost every aspect of making a film, for practical purposes and as artists who wanted to control the final product. These skills and knowledge made them all dynamic producers—they understood the resources and time they needed to get a great film made.

In today's world, virtually anyone with an iPhone and some free editing software can be a "filmmaker." There are people creating content online with minimal resources, but are they actually filmmakers? Have we devalued the craft by simplifying it to an ability to point, press a button, and cut together a few clips in a simple computer program? Have you ever wondered how there are so many "filmmakers" in the world today? To add to this question, the "suits" in the boardrooms often don't have a creative clue about the craft of filmmaking. Even being a film school graduate doesn't necessarily make you a good filmmaker

Contrasting the earliest filmmakers with today's filmmakers is easy. On most sets, there are people designated to carry cables from one place to another, and people who exclusively drive trucks from one place to another. Nobody else is allowed to touch those cables or trucks but those designated people. Is it impractical to operate this way? Have you ever seen a set filled with people standing around doing nothing? I have, many times.

Is this a sustainable way of making movies, especially for independent filmmakers? Businesses who offer products and services worldwide are in a constant operational trend of finding efficiencies that save money and time. This function allows product and service providers to be more competitive. Whether we want to accept it or not, we are in an economic contraction. How can filmmakers compete in a global market? Spend the least amount making the best film possible; this is the ultimate X Factor for us, the unknown variable that everyone in our industry is continuously trying to figure out. And it's a moving target.

Will independent film sets have crew members standing around doing nothing in ten years? Will this overarching trend continue? Is it important to find efficiencies and preserve resources? We must go back to basics to sustain ourselves as filmmakers. This overinflated structure is the very definition of an economic bubble, and I don't believe it is sustainable. Most economic challenges can be addressed with a basic acceptance of the laws of supply and demand. Why do most independent films lose money? As filmmakers, we are facing a challenge to make a product that, at the very least, recoups the capital it cost to make. Most monetization opportunities are grossly out of alignment with the cost of the product, so, in addition to improving distribution strategies and business models, we must look at the costs of making the film. Our survival as independent filmmakers is much more important than following the industry "standards" that dictate who carries a cable from one place to another. If we do not change the way we make movies, we risk becoming obsolete. This concept is not an idealized fantasy. It is an economic reality.

It is your job as a filmmaker to master the craft. I realize it is unrealistic to expect anyone to do what Georges Méliès did, but imagine a producer who is fluent in the gaffer's terminology, cables, lights, grip, and electric. Consider the producer who understands cinematography, editorial, or color. A producer who understands the technical, creative, practical, *and business* sides of filmmaking will rise to the top. Some of the most memorable films of our time were made with meager budgets by bootstrapping resources with directors serving multiple roles on set and in post-production.

Make learning every aspect of filmmaking (especially business) your top priority. You don't have to be an expert at everything, but you should understand the fundamentals of each department on your set. Become a master of your craft, and it will show in your work and everything you say and do. Remember, always be a producer first. In this case, a producer who is a master of every aspect of their craft.

Henry Ford famously said, "I have a row of electric push-buttons on my desk, and by pushing the right button, I can summon to my aid men who can answer any question I desire to ask concerning the business to which I am devoting most of my efforts." It is critical that you build what Napoleon Hill called a Mastermind Alliance with likeminded people who are better than you at doing what you need them to do.

Everything you want to learn is available at your fingertips. Search out and find online videos, blogs, books, and local classes and workshops. There are cinema cameras that are considered industry standard, like the Red camera. I own three of them, and when I bought them, I knew enough basic operations to run them, but I wanted to master my tools at a different level. I decided that, prior to directing my first film, I would attend a week-long event called "Reducation," a class sponsored by Red Digital Cinema, the company that makes the cameras. This was an intensive program led by industry experts, and it covered the entire workflow from image capture to post-production.

There were several occasions on the set of my film when I knew more about troubleshooting the cameras than anyone in the camera department. My impression was that I was taking this training in an effort to keep up with the experts in the camera department, but to my surprise, my technical knowledge exceeded theirs. I don't believe technical knowledge replaces creativity or talent. I do, however, believe that, as producer, I was able to save time and resources by quickly troubleshooting the cameras onset instead of having to bring in outside help that could have cost us hours of time. I have done the same thing with almost every function of production and post-production, my level of knowledge is enough to carry on a meaningful conversation with anyone in those departments.

More importantly, master the business side of production. Gain a level of knowledge that allows you to provide potential investors and peers value through education. Beyond just finance and investment, help them understand the legal aspects of production. Gain a basic understanding of intellectual property laws pertaining to screenplays and finished films. Understand the talent, property, and location releases you will need while in production. Understand the contracts that you will be signing with the investor, service providers, and crew or labor unions.

Be a producer who is a master of their craft, and you will gain the results you seek.

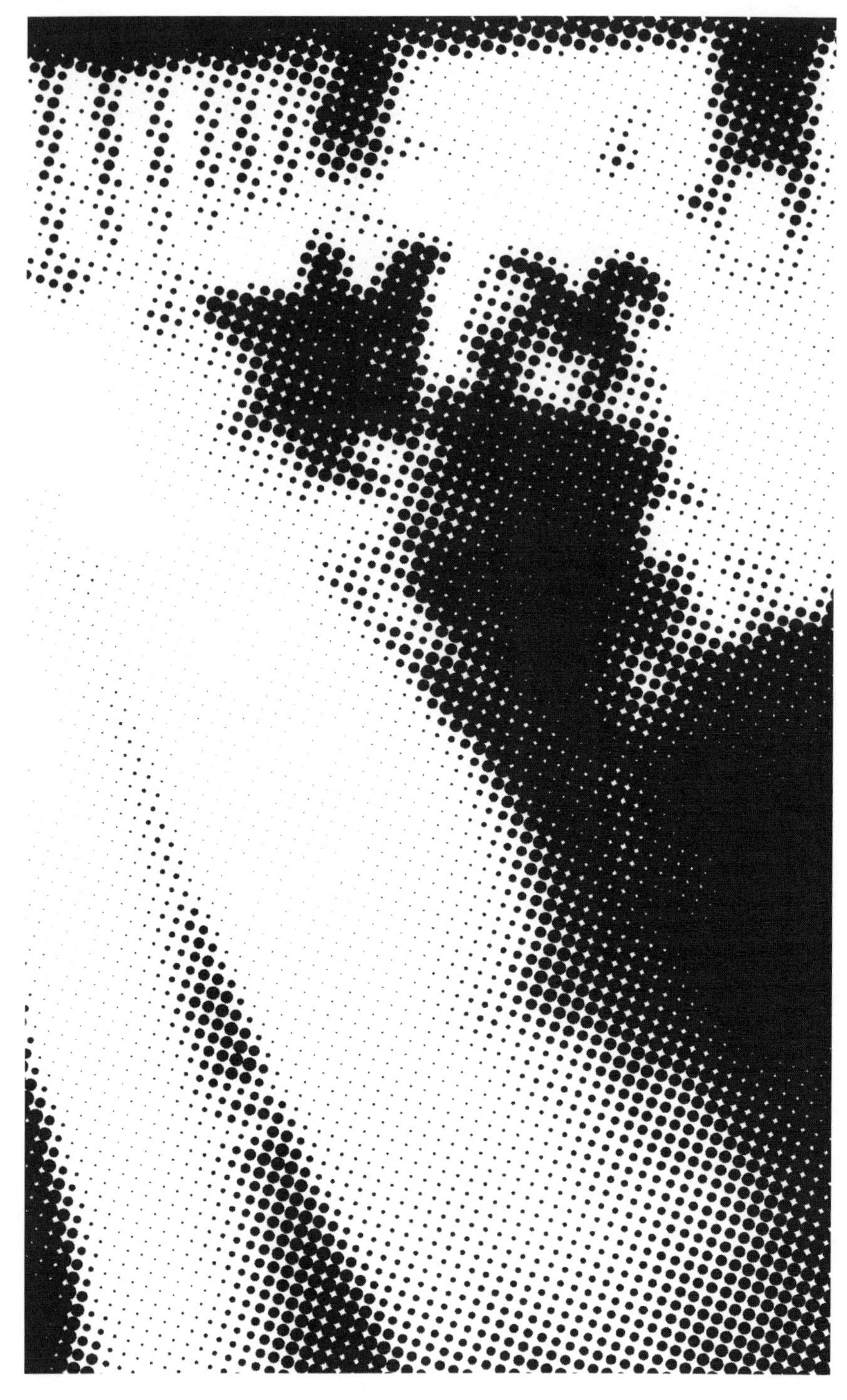

CHAPTER ELEVEN

SELLING YOUR SOUL TO THE DEVIL

*"I would travel down to Hell and wrestle a film
away from the devil if it was necessary."*

—Werner Herzog

It is critically important to be confident in what you know and what you have to offer. Make sure you are speaking with investors at their level. You are not beneath them in any way, and chances are, they are not smarter than you. Command respect with excellent communication and the expertise of the film industry, and as a professional who has mastered the craft. You're not selling investors anything, so be cautious not to sell too hard with your pitch or you will give them the impression that you are desperate. Assume your investor is a shark who can smell desperation like a drop of blood in the water a mile away.

Some investors will prey on desperation. They will try and take more than what most investors ask for, and they will put you under very stringent terms. It is not necessary to sell your soul to the devil to make a film, but that decision is yours to make on a case-by-case basis. A great example of a very shrewd investor is Kevin O'Leary on the TV show *Shark Tank*. Kevin is brilliant at putting himself precisely where the money opportunity is while obligating you for a very long time. He seems to prey heavily on those who are desperate for capital, and is generally denied by those who are confident in who they are and what they have.

Later in this book, you will read another example of a deal I had with a major Chinese media company, showing another way investors will often push for much more. Sometimes it's a cultural way of doing business, and sometimes it's just greed. The rule in negotiating with an investor is simple: the investor is holding all the cards, and they know it, but you should never set yourself up to fail. Be realistic about what you can commit. Whenever possible, you should under-promise and over-deliver. This practice will establish an excellent long-term relationship with the investor and leave the door open for future projects.

Think five steps ahead. If your means to an end is getting the film financed at any cost, you will get yourself into a pickle and likely not meet your obligations. Think about what your next steps look like. If you've never managed post-production and delivery, speak with someone who has and get a realistic and practical timeline and budget to see what you will need. Never plan for the best-case scenario; in fact, you should almost ALWAYS prepare for the worst-case scenario because the only direction to go from there is up.

Do not allow the investor to take any authority away from you. Too many times, there is a misalignment in responsibility and authority, and that will never work. If you have an obligation to deliver a quality film, you should have the authority to carry out anything to make that happen, as long as it is in the best interest of the project. Investors will respect you for taking a stand. This practice is the act of a leader in control.

Depending on the investor's level of experience in the film business, he or she may be expecting an Academy Award or Brad Pitt and Angelina Jolie as leads in your $500,000 film. You need to set very clear goals in pre-production, production, and post-production. It would be best if you defined everyone's expectations with casting as early as possible so there are no surprises. Remember, under promise and over-deliver. You have the power to control your success by defining it ahead of time. Do not let your investor pressure you into committing to a big cast or anything else not under your direct control. A good producer is realistic with managing their investor's expectations.

Defining success is a critical part of making your deal, so do not be bashful or afraid to assert your authority. If you were taking a cruise out to sea and met the captain of the ship, would you not expect the captain to tell you everything you need to know about the trip at sea? Would it make you comfortable if the captain said, "Sure we can do it your way instead"? No. So why would you change the way you sail your ship? Be the captain of your film. You have the responsibility to deliver a quality product, and you need to show everyone involved that you have the authority and mastery to do it.

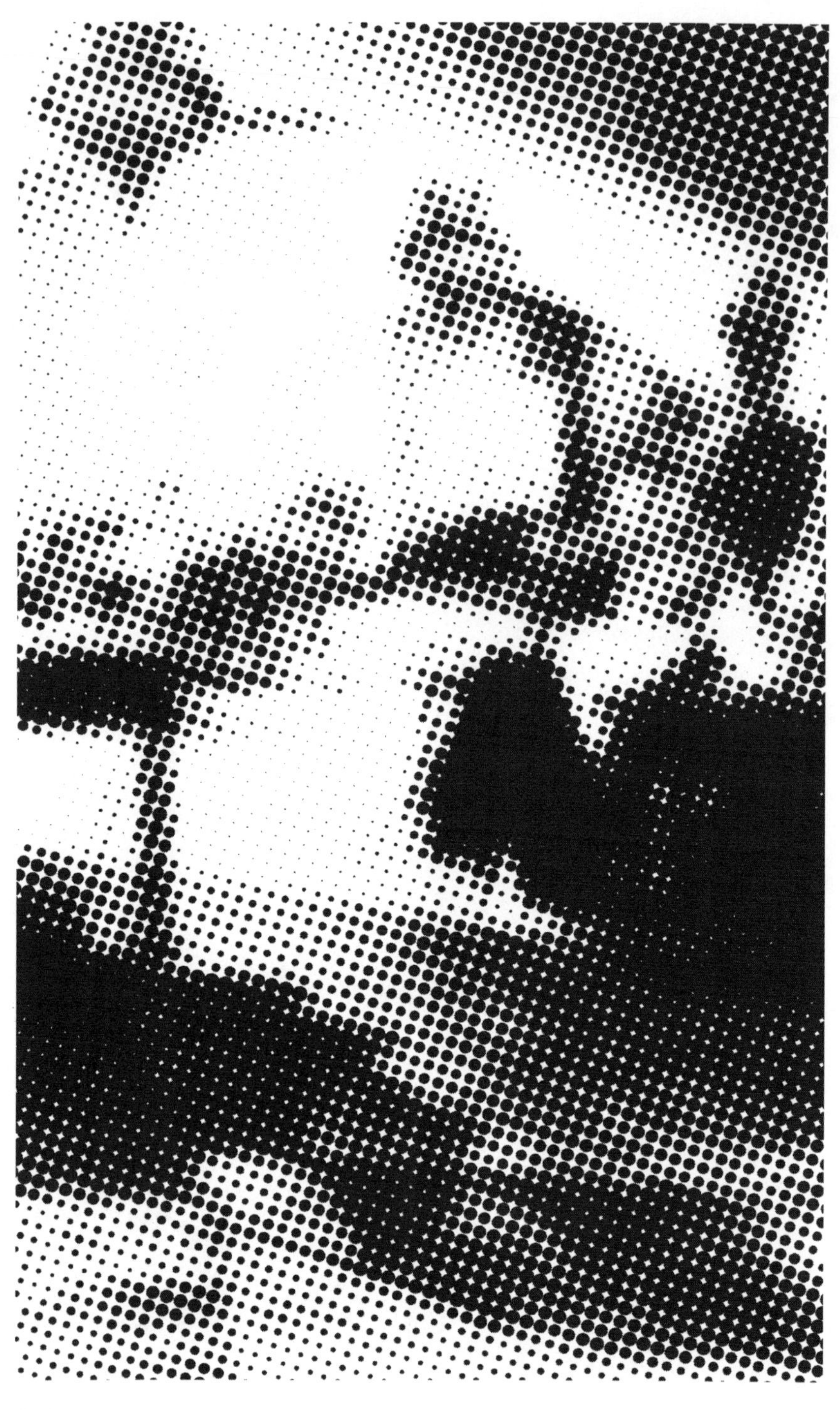

CHAPTER TWELVE

IF IT'S NOT YES, IT'S NO

"Drama is life with the dull bits cut out."

—Alfred Hitchcock

A very successful mentor once gave me lots of great advice, but two items in particular are important to mention in this book. The first was what he called the definition of happiness: "living in a house that is paid for, and having money in the bank and a daily bowel movement." I found this to be very accurate. The other advice he gave me was even simpler: "There are only two answers in the world: YES, and everything else is NO." This concept took me years to truly understand, but after wasting so much time with some of the colorful characters I've written about in this book, I realized what he meant. And I continue to learn it every day.

If you've tried to raise money for a production, you have no doubt experienced the paralysis that comes from indecisive people. For some reason, some people get pleasure from spending their time wasting other people's time. I don't know what it is about these people. Maybe it's the temporary validation that someone takes them seriously, or perhaps it's that they are just narcissistic and feed on people who respond to the carrots they dangle. However, this one piece of advice that this successful man gave me can quickly eliminate most of those people for all of us.

There are countless examples of producers who meet "investors." Sometimes these people have money and for some reason, they like to surround themselves with people who want something from them. In some cases, they will say "YES" to you, and then string you along for months. You'll discover only later that they never had any intention of investing in your film and it was all just a waste of time. Other times, you'll discover they simply have nothing to give, and they are just full of shit.

Years ago, I set a meeting with an "investor" who drove up in a shiny new Rolls Royce. He popped out of the driver seat with his long ponytail swinging around his tacky jumpsuit and gold chains glistening through his chest hair and said, "Are you Albert?" His assistant, who acted more like the mother of a toddler, swiftly jumped out of the passenger seat with a notebook as if she wanted to make sure he didn't do or say anything stupid without her being there to clean it up. He spent our entire visit boasting about how much money he had, and even went so far as to show me a check that he pulled from his back pocket like a magician. The check was written to him for $2,500,000. He said yes to everything I pitched, and I wanted to believe I had just found financing for my projects, even if it was from the devil himself. After that, we exchanged a few emails. His were mostly cryptic and incoherent, but I thought to myself, *There's no way this guy doesn't have the money, he has a Rolls Royce and a ponytail.* Days turned to weeks and weeks turned to months before I realized he was full of shit and I had wasted lots of valuable time.

I have a friend who bought a nightclub in LA, and I decided to go to the club one Saturday night. I joined my friend for a smoke break outside. Moments later, what do you know? Mr. Ponytail swings into the valet in his shiny new Rolls Royce. My friend knew who he was and confided, "That guy is a joke and a complete con." I discovered he only rents that car to drive around town pretending to make movie deals while preying on young aspiring actresses. I was in shock, and I couldn't believe the extent people will go to, to play this bullshit out. This guy uses the money he earns in whatever he does for a living to rent a car and pretend to be someone he's not. This experience was a massive slap in the face for me, and I resented the fact that I had fallen into such an obvious trap. I realized at that moment that my desire to make my film had blinded me to the most obvious indications that this person was full of shit.

This story is a perfect segue to my next point. You will no doubt run down the rabbit hole with people and waste a lot of time and resources doing it. I have a stringent rule that I will now ask you to practice: DO NOT announce or talk about a project as if it is financed. DO NOT engage anyone or make any plans at all without money in the bank, free and clear with 100% exclusive access to the capital. I don't care if it is Bill Gates himself who says YES, there are a million things that can and will go wrong and will cause your house of cards to fall, even at the very last minute.

There's nothing more painful than hearing the stories of film-makers who raised part of their budgets and started production because they had commitments from other investors, only to have the rug pulled out from under them at the last minute. Not securing financing when you expect it will not only disrupt your project, but it will also cause you to lose credibility and may even get you sued for pulling out of deals you made while you were counting on that money.

DO NOT allow the desire to make your film blind you to this rule. There are only two answers: YES, and everything else is NO, period. There are no exceptions to this rule: YES means that you are engaging an attorney or negotiating a term sheet with your new investor and moving things forward. If you feel that someone is stringing you along, you're probably right. If that's the case, pass the burden on to them, and move on. You can politely tell them to circle back to you when they are 100% ready to move forward. If they are serious about investing with you, they will come back. If they are full of shit, they will never come back, and you will have moved on and saved yourself from wasting more time.

I was once contacted by a representative of a Korean tech company who had an interest in financing independent films. I checked the company out, believed them to be legitimate, and decided to take a meeting with them in their L.A. office. We met in a Wilshire Boulevard high rise, and I sat through their presentation on 3D technologies and heard all about the chairman who was coming to L.A. soon and wanted to meet film production companies for a possible partnership. Wow! This was the kind of stuff I had read about in the business trades—finally, a real business opportunity with an Asian company.

Weeks went by, and we set a meeting with the chairman, who didn't speak a word of English but somehow had a degree from an American Ivy League school listed in his bio. We met at their offices and sat through the painfully extended version of the same presentation. This time, everyone was jumpy and nervous and had their best suits on. They were on their best behavior in front of the chairman and awkwardly laughed at all of his jokes, which we couldn't understand, even after the translator told us what he'd said. We had what we thought was a great meeting talking about something, but I wasn't entirely sure what it was yet. Then we found out the chairman had made dinner plans for everyone at the best Korean restaurant in L.A., so we proceeded to the restaurant, and they started bringing out course after course of amazing Korean food. The chairman kept ordering rounds of soju between taking group photos. Soju is similar to sake and can sneak up on you if you're not careful. Some of his employees were getting shit-faced, and they thought it was hilarious. Thankfully, the training from my college years kicked in, and I was able to pace myself and hold down the alcohol without altering my perception of what was going on. We spent the night talking about business at a very theoretical level. No details, no numbers, no real actionable follow-up items. Eventually, the translator was so drunk that we lost all communication with everyone, and the evening became a series of awkward laughter and slurred sounds.

The plan was that we were going to do something huge, only no one at the table had any idea what it would be. I decided to enjoy the great Korean food, soju, and awkward laughter, and I parked my logic for the evening. The days ahead were filled with requests for detailed business plans, marketing plans, and operating budgets to produce a slate of films. I was working in the dark because I had no idea what they wanted. Being the obsessive professional that I am, I proceeded to work my ass off to develop these documents in a general way as quickly as possible and send them to the Korean executives in hopes that it would start a detailed discussion or that something substantial would come of it. When I develop business plans, I don't cut corners; these reports were outstanding and highly accurate.

They eventually went radio-silent, and I thought, *Sometimes no news is good news. Maybe this is the way Koreans do business.* We ultimately heard back weeks later, when they told us the chairman was coming back to L.A. and had requested we join him for a golf game to continue the discussion and planning. I thought, *This is great!* My golf game is pretty bad, but I figured that would give the chairman the satisfaction of beating me. We made plans to join him and his team, and we had a tee time and location at a high-end private country club. The day before the big game, the representative called and asked if I could bring a movie star with me. *What? A movie star? What the hell is going on?*

I decided, way too late, to dig a little deeper. I found the executive's social media feeds online and put the puzzle pieces together. It turned out this company was a publicly traded company in Korea, and they raise money by selling stocks when they make announcements in the Korean business news. I discovered they had used all of my plans as their own to promote a new Korean film company in L.A., and they had made no reference to my company for any of it. I realized the chairman would come to L.A. for photo ops so he could post them on their news feeds to legitimize the announcements and raise money by selling stock. No bullshit, this actually happened. To this day, this company has not done anything they talked about doing many years ago.

It is so important to understand the difference between YES and everything else. It is so easy to fall into these traps because often, they are perpetrated by people who seem legitimate in every way. Sometimes they even wine and dine you and use innocent intermediaries. I have even had people fully commit to financing, and then disappear into thin air. DO NOT count anything as done until the money is in your account free and clear.

To complicate things even more, sometimes "yes" means no.

Another high-profile industry associate invited me to a breakfast meeting with a "VIP" from China who was looking for companies to invest in for the development of some Chinese-American co-productions. I took the meeting and met the woman and my associate at Cecconi's in West Hollywood. It was a lovely day sitting on the patio, and the woman from China was pleasant and seemed very eager to make a connection with someone who could help her launch this initiative. Unlike other meetings, we discussed what a deal might look like, and she explained to me that the Chinese media company would always need the majority stake and would only consider investing if we gave them 51%. The initiative involved a multi-million dollar partnership for the development of culturally relevant film and TV content targeted to English-language audiences.

The discussion rapidly evolved into what would be a deeper business relationship, we agreed on broad terms, and I prepared a term sheet and emailed it to her as she requested. At this point, she was back in China, and our communications were limited to email. She told me that she would review the terms and make a recommendation to the media company officials. Her next round of emails indicated that they were ready to make a deal, but they wanted 60% instead of 51%. Now, anyone in my position would be a fool to pass up this opportunity over 9% when someone is willing to finance a business venture of this magnitude, so I agreed to move forward with this understanding.

Weeks went by, and I finally heard back when she sent me a revised term sheet. To my surprise, they had turned all the terms inside out and had reduced me to an employee of a production company owned by the Chinese media company, with 5% of something that I didn't understand. Now, I have no idea how I went from being a principal and producer with 40% ownership to an employee with 5% ownership of nothing. I won't put you through the pain of hearing every detail, but I want you to understand how deep these shades of gray can go. I had a deal with a major Chinese media company, and it fell apart after six months of development. The first round of financing was going to be $8,000,000, and we had written and verbal agreements in place until the very last minute. This two-step nonsense can happen to anyone, and it does. It is a normal part of doing business. Remember, I had gotten the "yes" to all the terms—more than once—and it still fell apart. So don't be discouraged if you waste time. It is inevitably going to happen.

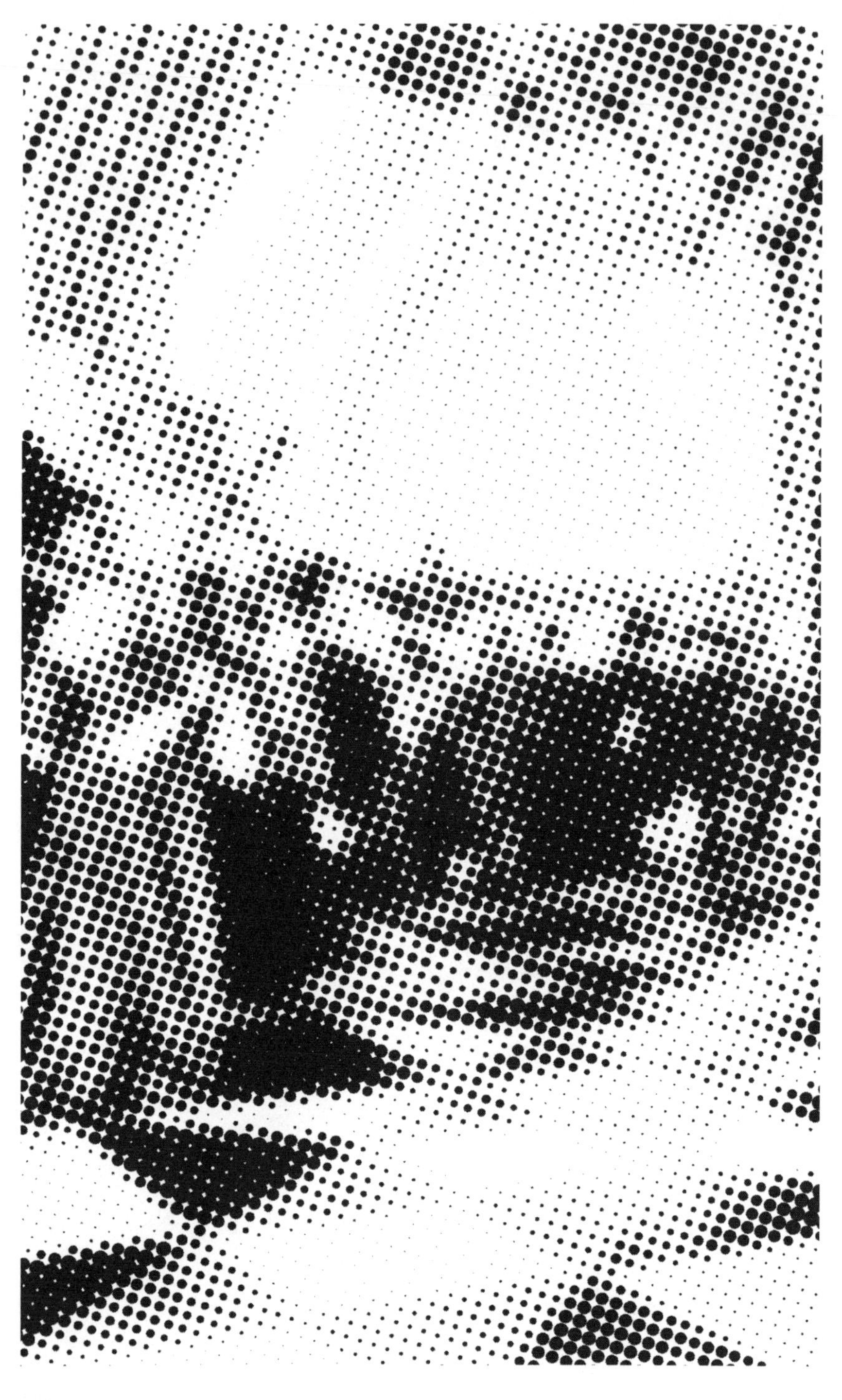

CHAPTER THIRTEEN

GETTING THE INK

"The Only Safe Thing is to Take a Chance."

—MIKE NICHOLS

There are many ways to formalize the deal, but you should be ready to plug in some proper nouns and numbers at all times, even if it's just a term sheet to get things started. Have an attorney lined up and ready to spring into action. The investor will likely ask you to provide the agreements for them to review.

You should develop (with your attorney) a rock-solid term sheet that you can send out to investors within 24 hours. This will assist in making certain you are all on the same page before drafting a long-form agreement, and it is usually easier for an investor to review the terms at a glance instead of filling their email box with long contracts. This doesn't mean you shouldn't have the longform template ready to go, but utilizing a term sheet first will likely save you time. Make sure your attorney reviews everything (even the copy in your email) before sending anything to your new investor.

You should also send a copy of the script, budget, and shooting schedule—along with any other documentation you think will be helpful in showing how organized you are—in a separate email. Consider presenting your investor with a binder with tabs for each section. Create a nice label with the title of your production and your logo (if you have one).

Once, it took me six months to put together all the legal components to close a deal and get funded. I cannot stress enough how important it is to have this work already done, if possible, *before* you close a deal with an investor. You are the captain and the ambassador of this project, so take it by the reigns and drive it to the finish line. Be available 24/7 by email and phone to quickly react to any questions that may come up, as there will be many.

Always leave yourself the flexibility of bringing in other investors or taking more money from the same investor at any stage of production, but particularly at two critical stages. The first is when you have a rough cut after finishing principle photography, and the second is when your film is completed. This final stage will likely require a last-in/first-out position. Raising money at this stage is usually a slam dunk if your movie looks and sounds great. It is best to be upfront and open with your investor, utilizing a visual timeline that lays out a clear plan showing the stages of production and investments. You can also offer options for participating in your project at three stages as opposed to all upfront if the investments cover each step. I will caution you to be very careful with this strategy, as it can result in running out of money with an incomplete film. This is for those who have established relationships with their investors and can rely on both parties delivering on their promises. I highly advise against taking investments in stages if it is the first time you're doing business with this investor. You're better off waiting until you raise all the money you need to complete and deliver the film. Never let your desire to get the film made outweigh your logic and common sense.

Make sure you speak with your attorney and tax professional to understand how to structure any investment properly. It would be best to do that ahead of closing a deal, if possible. This practice will also show the investor that you have your shit together. Choose a good lawyer with experience in the business, someone who can also educate your investor if any questions come up. Again, expert-level mastery of the industry will reflect on you as a leader and on those you choose to work with on your project. I will never forget how frustrating it was the time I was stuck negotiating with a writer who was represented by a personal injury attorney in Florida. I eventually just gave up and told the writer to find an attorney with experience in our business. Be professional, and master your world. This is your business, and you are in control. Never show weakness, or you will make the investor feel like they may have made the wrong decision to invest in you. Be the leader they expect you to be, and help them through the process.

It is customary for the producer to pay the investor's legal fees that are incurred putting your deal together, so make sure you build that into your budget; anywhere from $5k-$15k should cover it, depending on who their attorney is and the time involved. For practical purposes, I would have the agreements notarized, and if your investor is out of town, utilize a reliable overnight service like UPS or FedEx. Leave nothing to chance, and cover every base you can think of. You are the producer and CEO of your film project, so it's time to step up and be the leader your investor expects you to be.

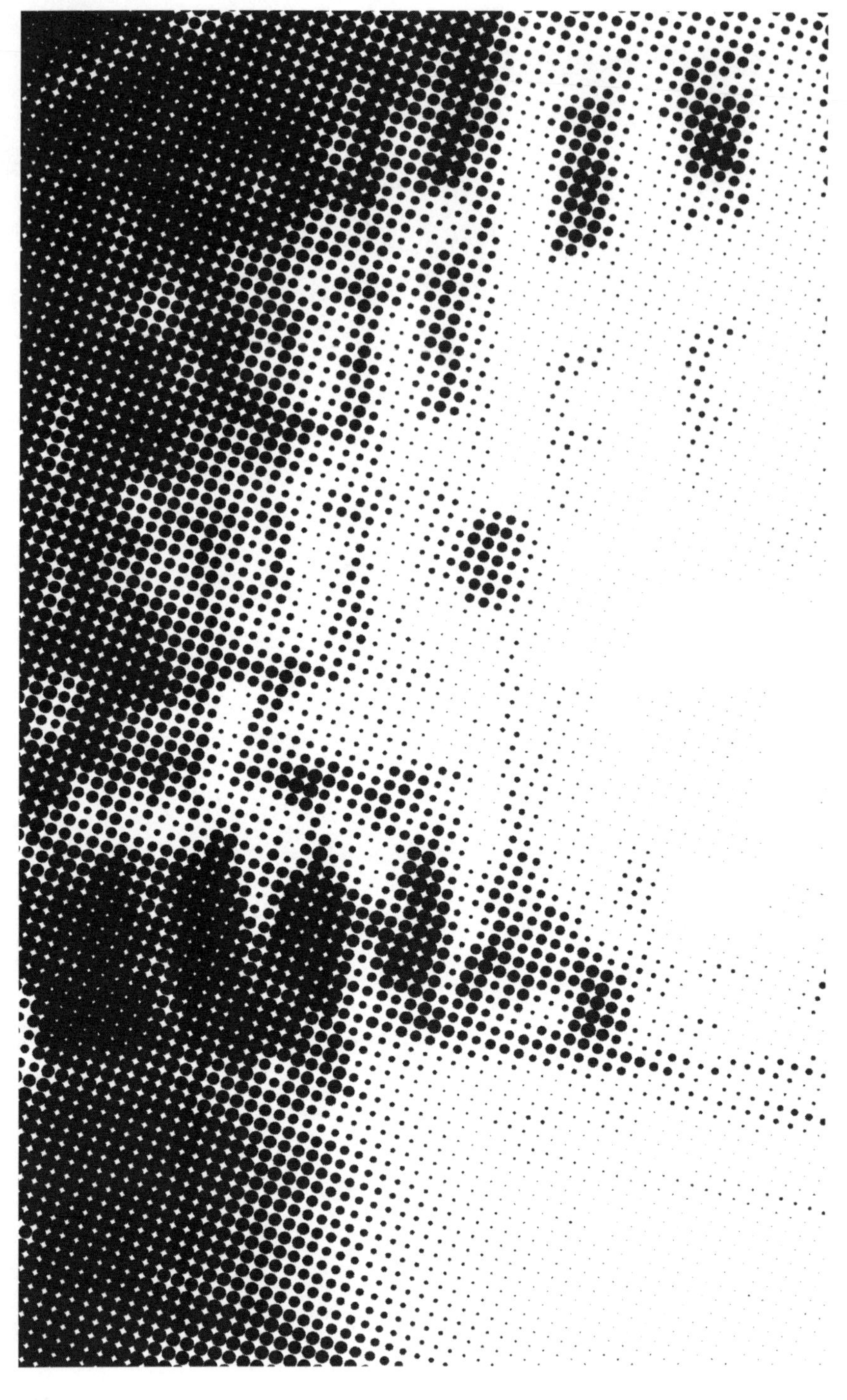

CHAPTER FOURTEEN

NURTURE THE RELATIONSHIP

"I'm like a navigator and I try to encourage our collaboration and find the best way that will produce fruit."

—Jim Jarmusch

Once you've been funded, assemble your team and put together a roles-and-responsibilities document with names and titles of your management team for your investor. Get in the habit of creating a weekly report, even if it's just a paragraph in an email. Report on your progress, and do not report minor problems unless you have to—and even then, not until after the issue has been resolved (as there will be many). If it's a big problem, you may need or want the investor's input. In that case, a phone call is best.

Do not be a high-maintenance business partner. Require only the very least amount of time from the investor, only what is absolutely necessary. Do not send them long emails or leave them long voicemails. Do not ask them lots of questions or ask them to provide you with anything you can figure out on your own. Be proactive and search for what you need on your own, and with the least amount of involvement from the investor (unless, of course, your investor wants to be more involved, as I discussed in Chapter 4). Make it as easy as possible for them to invest in you and your projects—answer their calls, texts, and emails 24/7.

In one of my productions, one of the lead actors was on a strict raw vegan diet. Three days into production, our first caterer got so upset with some of the dietary demands that they quit on us hours before lunch one random day. An assistant was sent on a two-hour roundtrip to pick up raw vegan food from the actor's favorite restaurant while the rest of us had a great new catering company providing everything else on time and budget. My producing partner handled everything without bothering me with it; he did, however, share it with me after it was all handled, and I think we had a good laugh. This story is an excellent example of a simple problem. You roll with it, find a solution, and keep moving forward. This problem could have been a major distraction to more than just one or two people, it could have blown up like a wildfire. Instead, my producing partner got on the phone and found a new catering company without any disruption to me or anyone else.

Do not copy the investor on general emails to your crew. You should, however, send the investor updated script drafts, updated schedules, call sheets, and any other physical production updates under a separate and private email from you with a brief explanation of what it is. In some cases, your investor may not want to see any of this, and that's great, but most of the time it makes them feel better to see their money in action. You should be the only point of contact for this information. Do not have anyone else communicating with your investor, and do not share your investor's name or contact information with anyone.

Do not take any shit from anyone. If any vendors or crew give you problems before you start filming, they will no doubt be ten times worse once filming begins. Get rid of them and move on—you do not need to increase your chances of additional issues during production. Believe me, you will have enough to deal with without these people. Problem people can take the whole ship down if you allow them. Your troops should respect you—if and when your investor comes to set, you must show him or her that you are in control and you run a buttoned-down operation.

It's important to keep your investor in the loop. If it's not too much burden on your production, try and post some dailies on a secure password-protected website, and send it to the investor so they can see the product taking shape. Don't send them anything that requires VFX or CGI or any green screen shots. Send them only the stuff that looks and sounds close to finished, if you can.

It's important to set boundaries early, and as such, try to limit the investor's set visits to pre-scheduled meetings. Make sure the investor understands that every single minute on set is scheduled for something. Time is literally money, and you have no "free" time to spare. If the investor wants to visit set during production, I would schedule the visit during a scene right before lunch so they can observe a scene being shot and then sit with you through lunch. As I warned before, there are some investors who will want to be on set every day. They will want a chair with their name on it, and they will want to assert their authority. These are all things that you should be prepared for before accepting money from anyone. Remember, the investor is your new business partner, and you should like them enough to tolerate them as much as they want to be around.

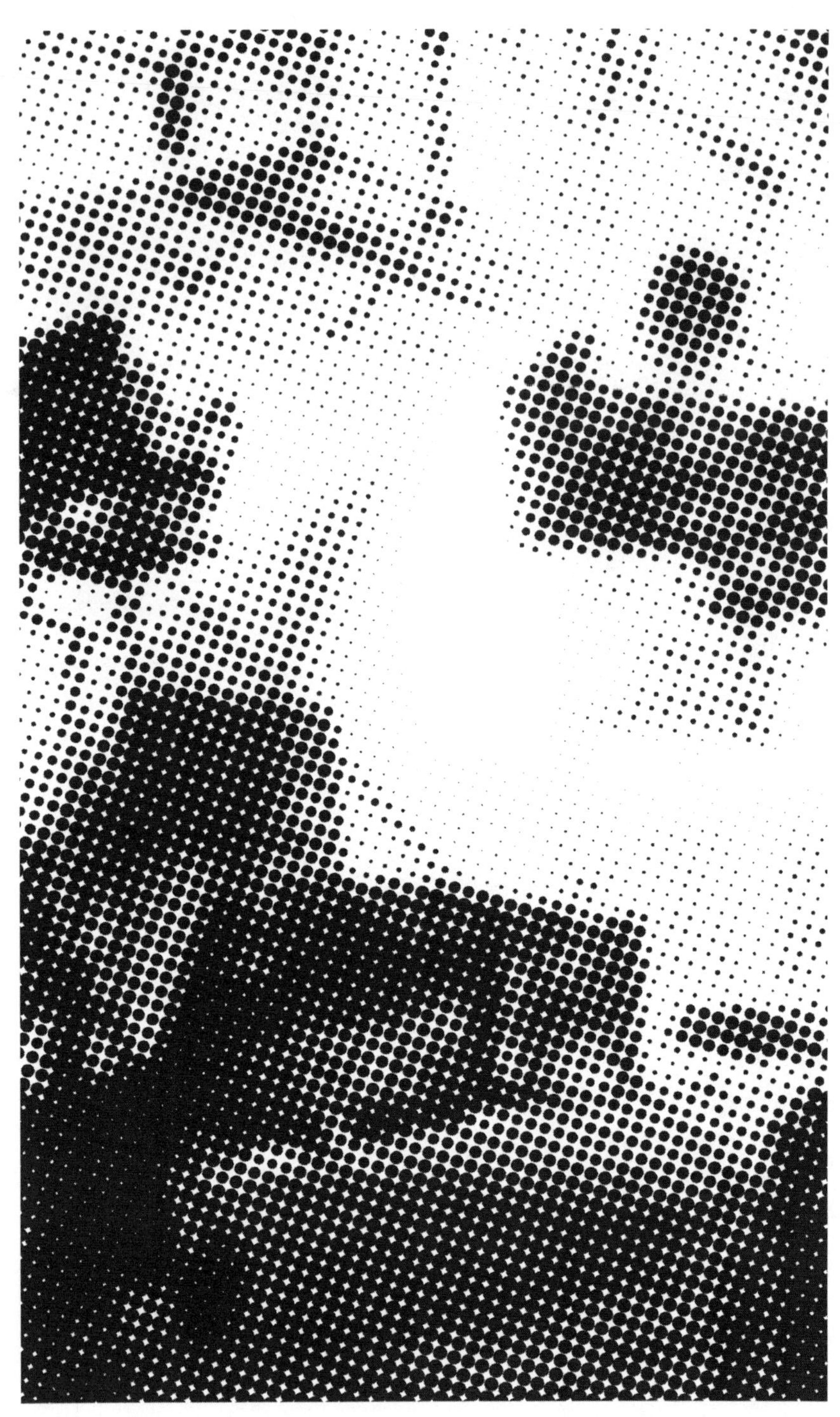

CHAPTER FIFTEEN

PAY NO ATTENTION TO THE MAN BEHIND THE CURTAIN

"The More Opinions You Have, the Less You See."

—WIM WENDERS

We have all been conditioned to believe that success is an outside force, available only to a select few. We subscribe to ideas like "the 1%," and by doing so, we create resistance and mental barriers for ourselves. Success exists within each one of us. It is our choice to manifest it into reality, or to continue to believe that it is only for the 1%.

Hollywood has always been a "walled garden," open to a select few who were either born into it or blazed their own trail. Yes, there is a certain amount of "right place, right time" luck, but if you're not taking action and getting out of your comfort zone, will you ever reach your right place? Success in this industry has little to do with "good" ideas. Yes, you heard me right: no one cares about your plans. There are thousands of great ideas floating around the industry, and everyone has listened to every one of them before.

Believe in yourself completely, and visualize what you want and where you want to be in the long term. Find a ritual or mantra that you tell yourself every day or maybe before a meeting. Get on the phone and make calls, break down barriers, and stop believing in the illusions that mainstream media feed us. What's the worst that can happen? Maybe you don't get a return call? Perhaps you get a "no"? Don't feel sorry for yourself; you are not a victim!

Perfection is paralysis, and waiting for the "right" time is what holds many of us back. The right time is now! "Waiting" for anything or anyone is the kiss of death in business. Don't wait. There is no tomorrow, only today. The only way you are going to make anything happen is by taking action right now.

I have yet to meet a successful business person who attributes their success to sitting around and waiting for the phone to ring. Every one of them took action. As imperfect as it may have been, they fought through adversity and found their paths. They all failed multiple times. Some even hit rock bottom and found the strength to pull themselves back up.

You *can* raise the money you need to make your film. It's entirely up to you. Don't subscribe to the victimhood culture. There are many examples of immigrants who came to this country with nothing. They believed in the American dream and found success by taking action despite their limitations.

It's your time to make history. Pick up the phone, and get out and take action today. There are many qualified investors waiting to connect with someone just like you, and they are ready, willing, and able to finance your film today.

Thank you for reading my book. I hope it helps you reach a new level in your journey.

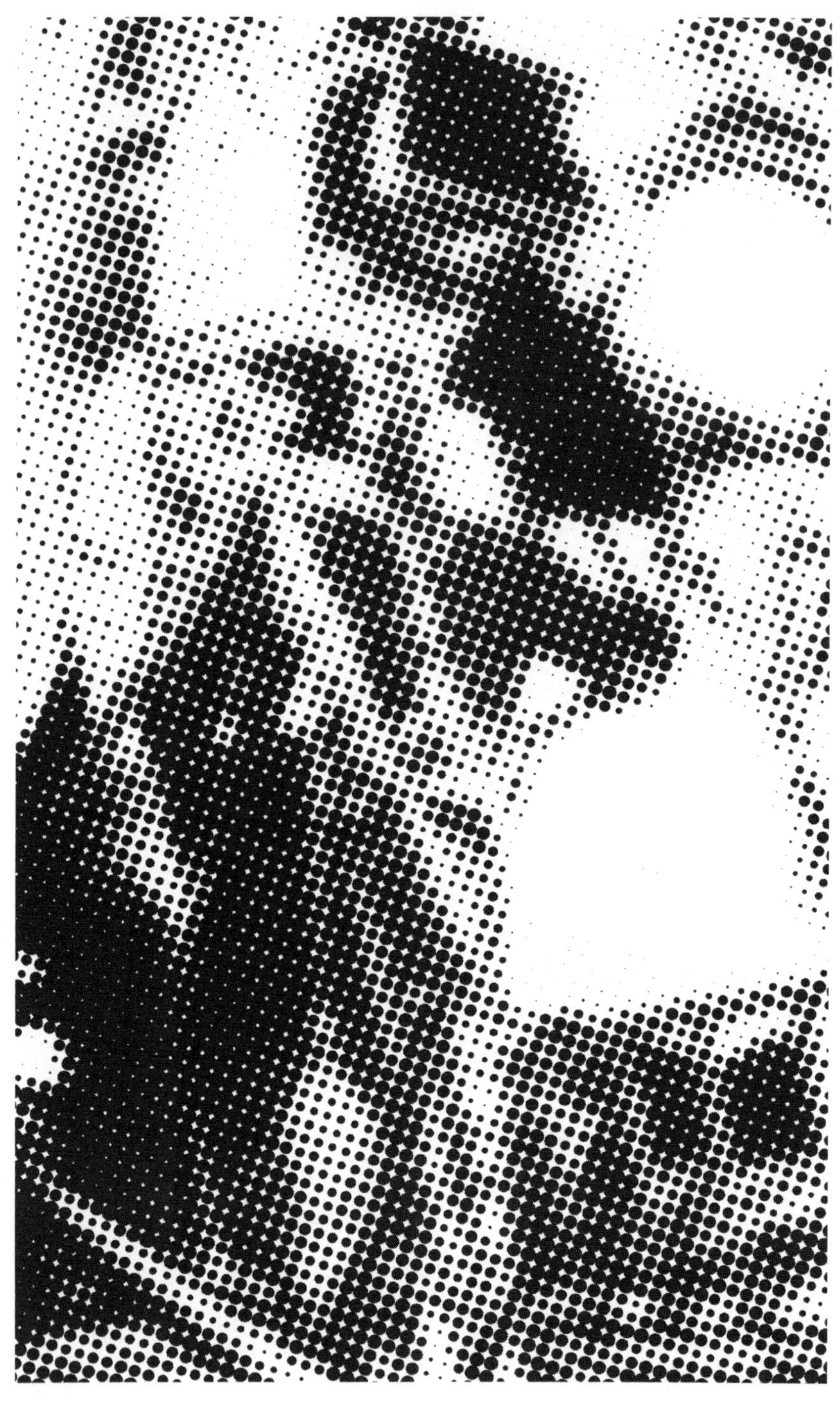

RECOMMENDED BOOKS AND OTHER RESOURCES

""Whatever the mind of man can conceive
and believe, it can achieve."

—Napoleon Hill

Think and Grow Rich

By: Napoleon Hill

I know what you're thinking: *How original.* Hahaha, yes, that's what I used to say, too—that is, until I immersed myself in the philosophy of Napoleon Hill and realized this was much more than just a motivational book. Read it with an open mind.

The Kid Stays in the Picture

By: Robert Evans

This is a classic Hollywood story about how a clothing salesmen from New York became a studio head and went on to make some of the most iconic films of our time. Robert Evans is one of my heroes.

The Art of the Deal

By: Donald Trump (long before he was president)

Don't get caught up in the fact that this was written by Donald Trump. Read it with an open mind, and you will gain incredible insight into how money people think and how there are many ways to get a deal done. Trust me.

Influence: The Psychology of Persuasion

By: Robert B. Cialdini

This book is a deep dive in how and why people say "yes." It's a great read for anyone in any kind of business development.

Your First 100 Million

By: Dan Peña

This book is not for the thin-skinned. Dan is a business drill sergeant with a no-nonsense approach. He takes no prisoners and does not subscribe to excuses or victimhood. He can be quite offensive, but if you are ready to understand the fundamentals of business, his strategies are among the best.

Never Split the Difference

By: Chris Voss

A former international hostage negotiator for the FBI offers a new, field-tested approach to high-stakes negotiations—whether in the boardroom or at home. An incredibly insightful book on so many levels.

The Business of Media Distribution

By: Jeffrey C. Ulin

This book is excellent, a comprehensive overview of the global distribution business. This is a great reference for understanding "traditional" media distribution as well as emerging models.

The Complete Film Production Handbook

By: Eve Light Honthaner

This is a must-read for anyone planning to produce a film. It's all about the nuts and bolts of almost everything related to physical production. Make sure you get the updated edition.

Film Production Management 101

By: Deborah Patz

Another perspective on the practical stuff. A thorough read filled with great information.

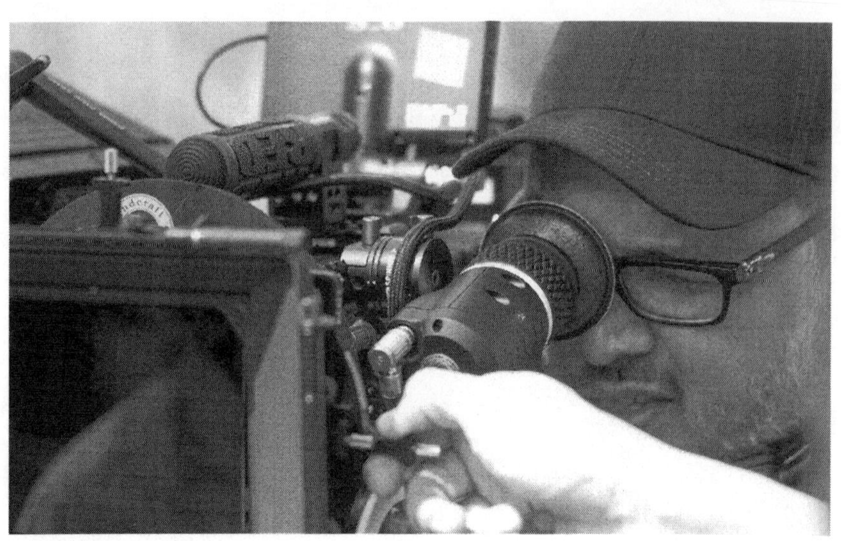

ABOUT THE AUTHOR

Part businessman, part artist, Albert Sandoval is a creative entrepreneur, investor, and filmmaker. His no-nonsense approach has earned him respect within the creative and business communities while attracting blue-chip affiliates and talent-rich collaborators. Sandoval is CEO of the production-distribution company RadioactiveGiant, a member of the Independent Film & Television Alliance, and an active participant in the global entertainment media business. He has served as executive producer on several feature films, and as lead producer on *Killing Winston Jones*, starring Richard Dreyfuss and Danny Glover. He produced and made his directorial debut with the psychological thriller *By the Rivers of Babylon*, starring Crispin Glover and Connie Stevens.

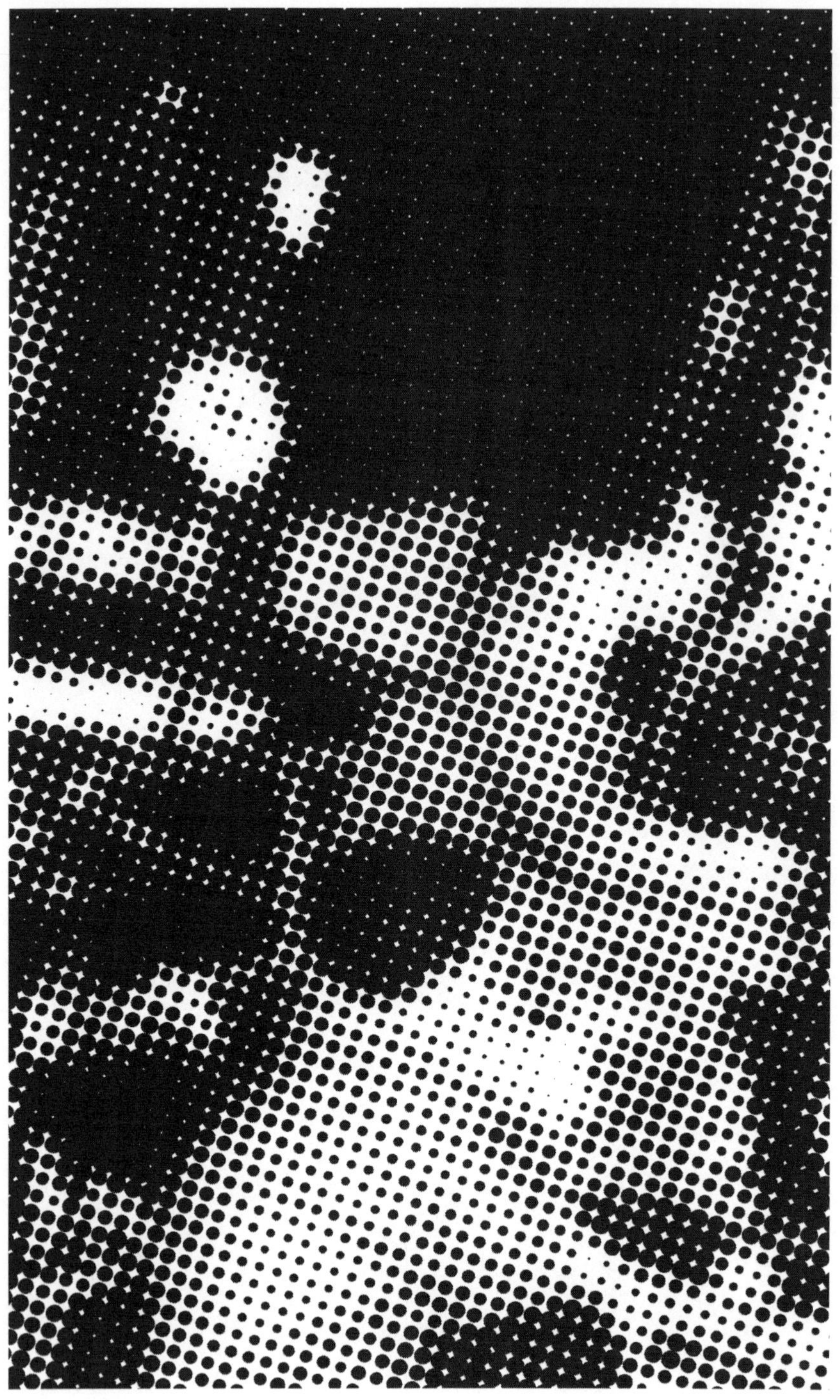

CONFESSIONS OF A FILM INVESTOR:
THE MISSING BOOK FOR INDEPENDENT FILMMAKERS

Private film investors are playing a critical role in the dawn of a new golden age of independent cinema. This book is intended to help filmmakers better understand these investors, or "money people." Follow the writer's journey deep inside his own search for investment opportunities with first-hand accounts and real experiences.

If you've ever struggled with finding real investors,
THIS BOOK IS FOR YOU.

If you've ever struggled with knowing how to effectively present yourself and your project, THIS BOOK IS FOR YOU.

If you've ever struggled to secure financing for your film productions, THIS BOOK IS FOR YOU.

Don't face the volatile world of film financing without reading this book.

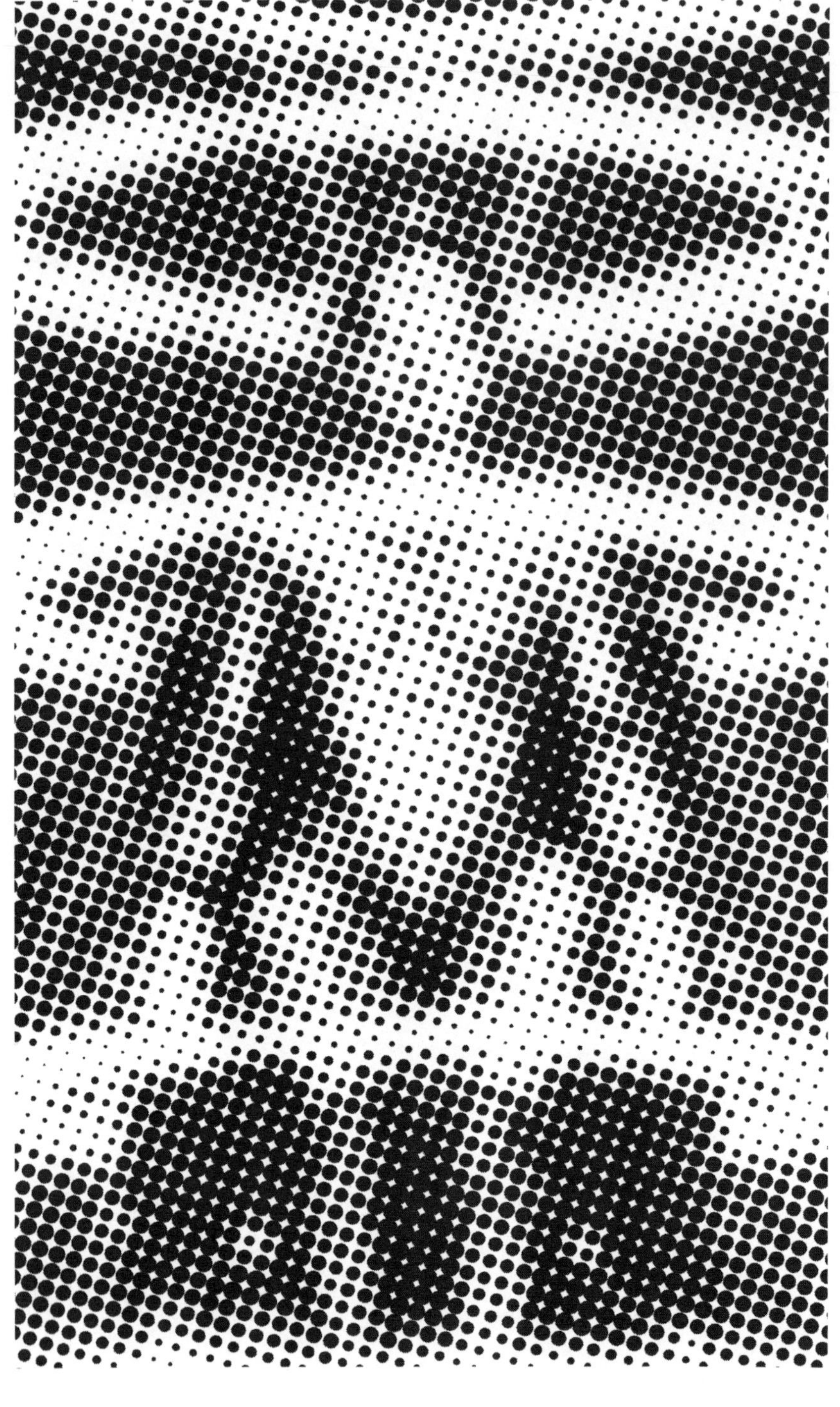

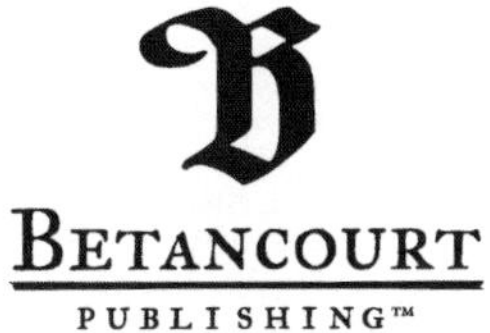

BETANCOURT PUBLISHING

An independent multimedia publishing company focused on development, curation, and distribution of unique and memorable works from artists, writers, and creators with unique perspectives and stories to share with the world.

www.BetancourtPublishing.com